The Heart of the Cross

Dr. Donald R. Downing

Mt Zion Ridge Press LLC
295 Gum Springs Rd, NW
Georgetown, TN 37366

https://www.mtzionridgepress.com

ISBN 13: 978-1-949564-93-8

Published in the United States of America
Publication Date: September 1, 2021

Editor-In-Chief: Michelle Levigne
Executive Editor: Tamera Lynn Kraft

Cover Art Copyright by Mt Zion Ridge Press LLC © 2021

All rights reserved. No portion of this book may be reproduced or transmitted in any form or by any electronic or mechanical means, including photocopying, recording or by any information retrieval and storage system without permission of the publisher.

Ebooks, audiobooks, and print books are *not* transferrable, either in whole or in part. As the purchaser or otherwise *lawful* recipient of this book, you have the right to enjoy the novel on your own computer or other device. Further distribution, copying, sharing, gifting or uploading is illegal and violates United States Copyright laws.
Pirating of books is illegal. Criminal Copyright Infringement, *including* infringement without monetary gain, may be investigated by the Federal Bureau of Investigation and is punishable by up to five years in federal prison and a fine of up to $250,000.

Names, characters and incidents depicted in this book are products of the author's imagination, or are used in a fictitious situation. Any resemblances to actual events, locations, organizations, incidents or persons – living or dead – are coincidental and beyond the intent of the author.

Unless stated otherwise, all scripture references come from the Scoffield Reference translation of the Bible, copyright 1909, Oxford University Press.

Table of Contents

Dedication   pg. 1
Preface: The Cup Before The Cross   pg. 3
A Communion Cup Before The Cross   pg. 7
Introduction: I Cross My Heart   pg. 13

Chapter 1:
A Look Upon My Face   pg. 19
    Facial Heart Expression
    The Cross of the Two Thieves
    Lift Him Up

Chapter 2:
The Heart of the Cross   pg. 33

Chapter 3:
The Blood and Water of the Cross   pg. 45

Chapter 4:
The Resurrection of Jesus Christ   pg. 63
    The Apostle Paul speaks of the resurrection
    He Has Risen!

Chapter 5:
The Bearing of Our Cross   pg. 71
    Crucified with Christ
    Deny Yourself, Take Up Your Cross and Follow Me
    State of Our Heart and Cross in a Sin Free Position
    Follow Me
    Bearing Our Cross to the Crossover

Chapter 6:
Contrasting the Cross of Jesus Christ and Our Cross   pg. 105
    Reviewing Contrasting Viewpoints of Our Cross and the Cross of Jesus Christ

Chapter 7:
Author's Journey to The Heart of the Cross pg. 117
    Author's Heart Biography:
    A Musical Experience
    The Cross Within My Doctor's Office
    The Man Beneath The Cross

Chapter 8:
Body Parts That Affect Every Believer's Heart pg. 131
    The Eyes
    The Mouth
    The Tongue
    The Lips
    The Ears

Chapter 9:
The Forensics of a Heavenly Heart pg. 137
    Heavenly Hearts
    Saved Hearts that Strengthen Heavenly Hearts
    The Forensics and Kingdom of Hellish Hearts
    Forensics of Lost Hearts that Support Hellish Hearts

The Ending pg. 147

Other Books by the Author pg. 149

Dedication

This book is respectfully dedicated to a great man of the Cross named Arthur Blessit, who physically carried a twelve-foot cross upon his back, walking all the way around the world. Many times he faced hatred, rejection, troubles, evils, and threats of death, yet he stood unmovable as a representative and demonstration of the Cross of Jesus Christ. As the messenger with a message from God for every ministry, he spoke to people in every nation about the cross he carried, regardless of the untold dangers and impossible odds that stood against him. He now holds the world record for physical cross bearing. Because of his passion, love, and faith in the gospel of the Cross, his historic words and works have been written upon the pages of time. *"The wooden cross that I have carried upon my back these many years is far less greater than the cross of Jesus Christ that lies deep within my heart."* (Heard on a TBN broadcast; date and program not remembered.)

Honor and thanks to Queen Almeta Bowman for the authorship of her book, *Finding the Inner Sanctuary*, that gives light, revelation, and the truth unto our inner man, including the mind as an entrance, the body, the soul and spirit as a sanctuary (sacred place, refuge, protection) and the heart as the most holy place, the place of forgiveness, love, God's word, faith, new life, and His earthly residence.

To my deceased wife, Lezlie Downing, who blessed me with twenty-three years of marriage and thirty years of ministry. And to my daughter, Stephanie, who blessed me on July 19, 2019 ,with a grandchild, Preston.

To the loving family of the late Elder Gregory C. Heyward, a man after God's own heart. Thank be to God for his heart, life and love for his church, family, friends, community, and the Gospel of Jesus Christ; spreading the message of the heart and being a blessing to Heart To Heart Christian Center for over thirty-two years.

To those who bow down and worship daily at the foot of the cross, who deny themselves daily to take up their cross and follow Christ with pure and clean hearts. You are God-approved through the *Heart of the Cross*.

Let us pray:
Father God, in the precious and matchless name of Jesus Christ, our Messiah, Lord, Savior, King, and Most Holy One. I thank You and praise You for giving me the grace and strength, and the opportunity to be a partaker of this book and the vessel You chose to use, to write it through me. I give You all the honor and glory and thank You for using me as Your messenger with a message of information, education, and revelation for Your body and bride, the Church.

Heavenly Father, that all who will read this book come to know the Cross of Your Son, His great love, compassion, grace, mercy, and forgiveness of sins, which was given to all mankind at Calvary, that all who believe, regardless of affiliate title or doctrine, will take up their cross of love, joy, peace, Your blood, word, and presence, and follow You. You are the only way, the truth, and the life.

I pray for prayer to increase for all lost sinners, for presidents, church leaders, the homeless, poor, homosexual, abortionists, and believers who have been deceived, misled, seduced by false doctrine and mammon, the "love of money" groups. Lord my God, we need more of You in the midst of every heart, marriage, family, and *The Heart of the Cross* in every ministry. As for me, that You will close Your ears to all the negative, wrong, and displeasing words from my mouth, every evil thought and wicked imagination of my heart, and give me eyes to see Your grace and presence, ears to hear Your voice, and a clean heart overflowing with Your love, word, shed blood, and faith.

Amen.

Preface:
The Cup Before The Cross

In the time frame (topography) of our earthly life, there are two basic cups available: a natural cup, which is finite (temporary), of man, and a spiritual cup which is infinite (eternal), of God. The cup of God and its contents are a good diet for our spiritual digestive system, which encompasses our mind, heart, body, soul, and spiritual life. A cup that contains vital nutrients and life concepts for godly living, growing in grace, understanding, revelation, wisdom, and knowledge of the *Heart of the Cross*. God's voice speaks unto all, in every nation from the infinite cup of His love, grace, mercy, and great heart, saying; *"Come and dine! Drink from My cup and be saved, drink to the full and be satisfied and approved of Me!"*

Now is the season for all to go forth and feast from the Lord's table, drinking deeply and daily from His cup of grace and salvation (Ps. 116:13) that is always full, overflowing like a river with love, salvation, faith, the word of truth, endless blessings, and revelation. Habitually (customarily), we view a cup to be an open container, like a small bowl or a natural vessel to drink from. Because of the cup of the Cross of Jesus Christ, we must also view a cup to be spiritual, our portion and walk of life; our call of God, our share, allotment of both our natural and spiritual existence imposed upon us as a cup to bear and drink of. The strength and fullness of a blessed life, the believer's cup is good, beneficial, and holy. For unbelievers, it is bitter, sinful, painful and wrong, propelling its victims into a lifestyle that leads to Satan's cup, his evil kingdom of darkness, hell, and eternal condemnation. At the young age of twelve, Jesus spoke to Mary, His mother, saying: *"Know ye not that I must be about my Father's business?"* (Jn. 18:11) (See Lk. 2:49) He knew in due time His cup would be finished on Calvary, He would have to drink of a bitter cup, containing all sin, sickness, disease, death, and even complete separation from God His Father (Jn. 12:27 and 18:37). On that dreadful and momentous day as He went forth unto the cup of His cross, He would cry unto His Father in prayer, saying: *"Father, if thou be willing, remove <u>this cup</u> from me; nevertheless, not my will, but thine be done."* (Lk. 22:42) (See Mk. 14:34-36) Though He was the Lord, our Savior, King, God's only begotten Son, He would have to drink from the godless cup of Satan's creation to save the lost souls of mankind, that our cup may be full of His word, blood, righteousness, truth, wisdom, and salvation of life.

In Psalm 75:8, David saw the cup of Jesus Christ and wrote this, saying: *"In the Lord's hands there is a cup. I will take the cup of salvation and call upon the name of the Lord."* (See Ps. 116:3 and Is. 53:1-12) Believers today are cupbearers who must drink daily of the cup of the Cross of Jesus Christ, wherein lies our redemption, salvation, and remission of sins. We cannot drink the cup of the Lord and the cup of devils, neither be partakers of the Lord's table, and the table of demons. However, there are several cups of the Lord that we His cupbearers must drink from:

A. The cup of God's salvation (Ps. 116:3)
B. The cup of blessing (1 Cor. 10:16)
C. The cup of the Lord's consolation (comfort, compassion, pity, and sympathy) (Jer. 16:7)
D. The cup of His word, blood, prayer, revelation and truth. We drink daily of Him. He is our drink offering. (Jn. 6:53-56 and 7:37)

Without the knowledge, salvation, and faith in the Cross of Jesus Christ, we shall surely drink of Satan's unclean cup, the cup of lost sinners, such as:

1. The cup of God's wrath and fury (Is. 51:17-22 and Rev. 16:19)
2. The cup of the devils (1 Cor. 10:21)
3. The cup of astonishment and desolation (Eze. 23:31-33)

These are all unclean (defiled, filthy, sinful, evil, nasty, and ungodly). Lost sinners drink of him, not knowing that he has not been washed (cleansed) in thousands of years. In speaking to the religious scribes and Pharisees, Christ spoke to them a parable of an unclean cup, a perfect illustration of the inner condition of their unclean hearts. While He spoke directly of an unclean cup, indirectly He was speaking of the negative state (condition) of their ungodly, hellish, and worthless hearts and lives.

"Woe unto you scribes and Pharisees, hypocrites! For you make clean the outside of the cup and of the platter, but within they are full of extortion (corruption) *and excess* (waste, dung, sins, refuse, stench, greed, and gluttony). *You blind Pharisee, cleanse first that which is within the cup and platter, that the outside of them may be clean also. Even so you also outwardly appear righteous unto men, but within, you are full of hypocrisy* (fraud, sham, mockery) *and iniquity* (wrong, unfair, evil doing, and immorality). *"* (Matt. 23:25-28)

All of them needed to repent of their ungodly cups, seek God for a new heart, a clean cup and a renewed mind. For they were all hell-bound through the doors of their church. The mind is the responding actor (aggressive, imaginative) and assertive, while the heart is the operative genius (master, discernment, power, and mastermind) of life, wherein lies our highest degree of intellectual capacity for godly (holy) living. They had great religious titles but poor, unclean hearts. Like many in leadership today, they were ignorant of the fact that our religious titles do not determine who we really are, but rather the heart and mind. The wisdom of Proverbs 16:9 teaches us, *"a man's heart deviseth* (plans, plots, creates, regulates) *his way, but the Lord directs* (conducts, guides, regulates, and supervises) *his steps."* For this we can always be sure He will give us the right cup, heart and mind, that we may be right, live right, do right, and enjoy an eternal place and a right position in glory.

A Communion Cup Before The Cross

As Jesus faced the cup of His cross, He gathered His disciples together for what is known as *The Last Supper*, customarily remembered by most churches as Holy Communion, using bread and wine in a cup to acknowledge the Son of God, His shed blood, His broken body and painful death. During Passover (a festival of blood), Jesus took His disciples into a small room and performed *The Last Supper* privately, using bread and wine. He held the communion cup that represented the fulfillment of His earthly life and the assurance that our sins would all be forgiven. He took bread, blessed it, and broke it and gave it to the disciples and said: *"Take, eat; this is my body."* And He took the cup, gave thanks and gave it to them and said: *"Drink ye all of it; for this is my blood of the new testament* (covenant, evidence) *which is shed for many for the remission* (pardon, forgiveness, mercy, and release) *of sins."* (Matt. 26:26-28). Christ spoke to His disciples during the Passover, revealing to them by Holy Communion that the bread for them to eat represented His broken body. The cup contained wine for them to drink, representing the blood of the New Testament, which would soon flow from *The Heart of the Cross*. He spoke plainly of the cup of His cross, saying: *"this cup is the new testament in my blood which is shed for you"* (Lk. 22:17-20).

The Lord's Supper (Last Supper) was a great love feast between Christ and His disciples the night before Jesus died on Calvary. Today we call The Lord's Supper, "Holy Communion," which is acceptable, but to our shame many fail to realize that Holy Communion requires holy (godly, pure), perfect, good, clean hearts and right minds. There is Holy Communion and holy communication, which are inseparable from holy hearts. We communicate with God individually and corporately as a celebration giving honor, thanks, songs of praise, rejoicing, shouting, dancing, and worship. Yet some do so with tears of repentance. There ought to be people getting saved, filled with the Holy Spirit, miracles, visitation of angels, and speaking in tongues unto God. Mankind often rejects what is acceptable to God. This occasion is not to be a fearful, morbid, symbolic ritual of remembrance. Have we failed to properly interpret the purpose, importance, and seriousness of the moment? I think so. God must be present! For without God's presence and approval it is a waste of time, a dishonor, a shame, and inappropriately out of order. The perpetrators are well worthy of the wrath of God. I say this because the <u>Lord must be there</u> in the midst of the hearts of His people (Hos. 11:9 and Matt. 18:20). Just as John the Baptist was a forerunner (predecessor, messenger) for Jesus Christ, Holy Communion is/was a forerunner for His Cross. Holy Communion also represents the fact that our sin debt was paid. There is no more curse in our lives. We have forgiveness of all sins. We are brought back into fellowship with God, redeemed, reconciled, and given a better commandment and covenant of grace and mercy. Jesus Christ was crucified on Calvary the very next day.

In 1 Corinthians 11:17-34, the Apostle Paul warns church leaders and communion takers about disorder at the <u>Lord's Table</u>.

1. There were divisions among them (Verse 18)
2. Some were eating the Lord's Supper as a meal, not leaving enough for others to eat and drink. Some dared to drink of the wine and became drunk. He scolded them for this great disorder (Verses 20-22)
3. In Luke 22:20 and 1 Corinthians 11:25, Christ revealed that the cup is the New Testament blood covenant, far above the law and the Ten Commandments (Heb. 10:14-18). This is a serious matter showing forth the *Heart of the Cross*.
4. In Verse 26-30, he explains that every time there is a gathering for Holy Communion, it was (is) to show the Lord's death until He comes. Those who are out of order

(taking of the Lord's cup) shall be guilty of the body and blood of the Lord, eating and drinking judgment unto themselves, not discerning the Lord's body (on the cross) and many shall become sick as unto sin and worthy of death.

For this, let us view the articles of Communion:

The Bread: In 1 Corinthians 10:16-17, the Apostle Paul showed forth his concern for the church at Corinth, saying; *"The cup is a blessing which we bless, is it not the communion of the blood of Christ?* (His blood on Calvary) *The bread which we break, it is not the communion of the body of Christ?* (Showing forth His bruised, broken and bleeding body) *For we being many are one bread and one body; for we are all partakers of that one bread."* Communion bread represents the body of Jesus Christ and His heart that was broken for us on Calvary. Jesus took bread and gave thanks, broke it, and gave it to them, saying: *"this is my body, which given for you; do this in <u>remembrance of me</u>."* Though breaking of bread shows forth the breaking of His heart, it fulfilled and finished His calling to the earth to heal the brokenhearted (Lk. 4:18-19). Bread is food for the living, sustenance, a sure and precious sustainer of life. Christ as the bread of God was/is also the Bread of Life. In John 6:22-48, the Lord confessed to the people and His disciples that He was/is the True Bread sent down from Heaven to give life unto the world, that whosoever comes to join Him shall never hunger or thirst. In verses 47-51, He said: *"Verily, verily, I say unto you, he that believeth in me hath everlasting Life. I am that Bread of Life. That a man may eat of it and not die but live forever."* Therefore, at every communion service, let us give thanks, honor, glory, worship and praise, showing forth our love and gratitude unto the Lord with all our hearts, minds, and souls.

The Blood: We read in Matthew 26:27-28 that our Lord took the cup, gave thanks and gave it to His disciplines, saying:

"Drink ye all of it. For this is <u>my blood</u> of the New Testament (covenant), *which is shed for the remission* (forgiveness, separation of) *sins."* As we look more seriously at the Eucharist Holy Communion cup in remembrance of the shed blood of Jesus Christ on Calvary, we remember that without the shedding of blood there is no remission (pardon, forgiveness, acquittal) of sins. Let us view some important things about the Communion cup of blood:
- We are justified by the blood of Jesus Christ (Rom. 5:9)
- We have faith in His blood (Rom. 3:25)
- Jesus washes the sins of believers clean in His own blood (Rev. 1:5, 1 Jn. 1:7).
- Our redemption is by His blood on Calvary (Eph. 1:7, Col. 1:14).
- We draw nigh (close) to God by His blood (Eph. 2:13).
- We have peace with God through the blood of His cross (Col. 1:20).

These are a few things we should remember as we hold the Communion Cup of Blood and wine in our hands. (Heb. 9:7 and 12-25, 10:4-19-29 and 13:11-12-20). By the shedding of the blood of the Lamb of God we were bought (purchased, acquired, paid for) with a price (1 Cor. 6:19-20 and 7:23, 1 Jn. 1:7). We became God's purchased possessions, having the right to partake of the blood and body of Jesus Christ. Being the life component of both our natural and spiritual hearts, the communion blood like unto communion bread is directly connected to the cross and given unto all from *The Heart of the Cross*. It assures us that we have a new and better covenant everlasting, a surety bond sealed with blood that cannot be annulled, wherein Jesus Christ is the mediator (arbitrator) of it (Heb. 12:24 and 13:20-21). It is eternal (Rev. 19:13).

The Wine: In John 2:1-11, we read about a marriage in Cana, of Galilee. Jesus and His disciples were called to the wedding. Among the Jewish people, a wedding was a joyous, festive occasion in which the whole community participated. Mary, the mother of Jesus, was there and when there wasn't any more wine, she took the problem to Jesus, saying: *"They have no wine."* Jesus commanded the servants of the wedding feast to fill six water pots with water and take it to the governor of the feast. The water that was made into wine tasted so good, the governor commended the bridegroom, saying how good it was, that he was being so wise he had saved the best wine for last. According to some scholars, this great wedding feast consisted of over 6,000 people. This was the first miracle that Jesus performed as the Son of God on earth (Jn. 2:1-10). In 1 Chronicles 9:29, the Levitical priests were appointed to supervise the oil and wine offerings of the House of God. The grape juice today hardly represents the blood of the Cross. As we drink of the <u>Cup of Wine</u> during Holy Communion, there are several things for us to think on in remembrance of Christ's blood shed for us on Calvary, His suffering, His death, and given life. God causes the grass to grow for cattle to eat, herbs to grow food for mankind, *and wine that maketh glad the heart of man* (Ps. 104:10-15). The Lord made oil, wine, and bread for us, yet not to be drunk with wine but to be filled with the Spirit (Eph. 5:18). When there is no sin in the heart, there will not be sin in the wine. God looks on the heart (1 Sam. 16:7). As a gift from God (Hos. 2:8), we are not to drink wine in excess (1 Tim. 3:8, Tit. 2:3 and 1 Pet. 4:3). The Apostle Paul instructed Timothy to *"drink no longer water,"* but use a little wine for thy stomach's sake and thy frequent infirmities (illness, ailments, weakness). In Mark 7:14-19, Jesus revealed that it's not what goes into us that defiles us, but what comes out of us from our hearts. We are instructed to give strong drink unto him that is ready to perish and wine unto those that are of a heavy heart (Pr. 31:6). In Genesis 14:18, Melchizedek (a type of Christ) brought wine and bread to Abraham. Jesus Himself did drink wine, and they called Him a winebibber, a drinker of much wine (Lk. 7:33-34), yet He was never drunk as a drunkard. Wine was used as a medicine (2 Sam. 16:2), as a sedative for people in distress (Pr.

31:6), pain, and suffering (Matt. 27:34, Mk. 15:23). In Luke 10:34, the Good Samaritan poured oil and wine upon the wounds of the injured traveler. There was no sin involved. Now we can better understand why by God's grace and mercy, pure wine is approved to be the best representative of the blood of the cross as we drink of it during Holy Communion, having pure minds and holy hearts, which is the most important thing.

Introduction: I Cross My Heart

As a young man, and even into adulthood, I cannot count the many times that I have taken my hand and made the sign of the cross upon my chest and boldly stated, *"I cross my heart and hope to die!"* Whenever we say these words unto others, or they say them unto us, we are stating assuredly that what we have said, done, will say, do, or believe is the honest truth. People worldwide, regardless of gender, race, or religion, cross their hearts and utter these words whenever there is a problem, situation, or issue of concern. Whether it's right or wrong in God's sight, I am not sure. However, I do believe *"and hope to die"* should never be spoken out of our mouths due to:

- **A:** The power of the words we speak
- **B:** The fact that life and death are in the power of our tongues (Pr. 18:21)
- **C:** Out of the heart our mouths speak, and Jesus came that we may have life. *I cross my heart.*

In Matthew 12:34-37, Jesus warns us about speaking empty words. *"O generations of Vipers, how can ye being evil, speak good things? For out of the abundance of the heart the mouth speaks. A good man out of the good treasure of the heart bringeth forth good things, and an evil man out of the evil treasure bringeth forth evil things. But I say to you that every idle word that men shall speak, they shall give account of it in the day of judgment. For by thy words thou shall be justified and by thy words thou shall be condemned."* (See Lk. 6:45)

In our bosoms we have a strong rib cage that covers and protects our natural heart and spiritually a breastplate of righteousness (Eph. 6:14) and of faith (1 Thess. 5:8) for our spiritual heart. People who use slang, idioms, useless, vain and futile expressions have no perceptions or knowledge of just how word- and cross-connected our hearts really are.

I am the founder of Heart to Heart Ministries and the overseer of great ministries, such as Redeeming Hearts Outreach Center (RHOC) under the direction of Pastor Michael and Markeet Lewis

(M and M), the school (and Heart) of the Jewish Prophets under the leadership of Apostle Margo Moore Valentine. As a fervent advocate, passionate for salvation, deliverance, and healing of man's heart, the Lord has used me to write many books about the *Gospel of the Heart* and to teach and preach many sermons about the *Cross of Jesus Christ*. Yet like unto thousands of other men and woman of the cloth, I viewed the body of Jesus as He hung on the cross and died, but <u>never saw His great heart</u>, the *Heart of the Cross*. I didn't understand the difference between preaching about the cross, and a real-to-life cross ministry to be lived by daily for life. When revelation came into my heart and soul that my heart ministry had to include the Cross of Jesus Christ, I became pricked in my heart. With guilt, shame, and often watery eyes, I began to write this book. God in His grace and mercy gave me strength when He spoke to me, saying: *"My son, the writer of the book is far more important unto Me than the book itself."* Like unto most authors, what I wanted (desired) most was a million-dollar book, but what I needed most was a million-dollar heart, firmly connected to the cross, by the heart of Jesus Christ. Though many authors write million-dollar books, many often sell just a few copies.

I cross my heart. Our faith (belief) in the cross, our hope and love in the cross, our salvation, redemption and resurrection by the cross are all predicated upon the heart just as the Gospel of Jesus Christ, the scriptures, prayer, love, faith, worship, the nine Fruits of the Spirit and the nine gifts of God, are all heart-operated. The blood that flowed down from the cross was clearly seen and yet behind that precious blood was a most holy, pure, loving and clean beating heart that would soon cease. No one dies until the heart stops beating. Let it be written upon every mind, heart, and soul that upon the hill of Mount Calvary the Lord Himself stopped His own heart from beating. He was the only one who could. The Lord said this: *"My Father loves me because I lay down my life, that I may take it again. No man taketh it from me, but I lay it down of myself. I have power to lay it down and to take it up again."* (Jn. 10:17-18)

I cross my heart that there are three crosses of utmost importance: our cross, the cross of the two thieves, and the Cross of Jesus Christ. All three are heart-predicated (asserted and declared), heart-operated (conducted and managed), performed, determined, and guided. For our spiritual prosperity, the Lord makes heart deposits, performs heart operations, and installs new hearts worldwide (Eze. 11:19-21 and 36:26). He knows there is nothing more valuable or precious in life than a beating heart, especially one that's been God-approved and faith-filled. A beating heart for Jesus Christ will never lose its value. We have the heart advantage by the Cross of Jesus Christ, benefits, blessings, helping support and God's approval. Not only is the cross a heart issue, but the heart itself is also a cross issue. Unknown to many, the heart is a blood, air and water pump, and the engine and womb of life, both natural and spiritual. It is the place of marriage, divorce, love, salvation, faith, and the Kingdom of God, wherein Jesus Christ rules as Lord, Savior, and King in the earth. Without a right, pure, and clean heart, even the cross of Jesus Christ has little meaning or eternal benefit.

I cross my heart. I have found the heart to be the seat of truth, virtue, honesty, and integrity. It also determines our character, victory, or defeat, our word vocabulary and daily conversation. It acts as our inner body furnace, our body temperature controller and distribution center. In the midst of sexual intimacy it determines our emotions, desires, feelings, and response. God loves every heart that contains His only begotten Son, His word and Spirit that work for the good of our life, salvation, mind, body, and soul. At this point please allow me to be honest, truthful, sincere, and most serious with you. The heart is the greatest prayer closet of spiritual life on earth. I cross my heart. One of the best things we can do when we pray is to lay our hearts at the foot of the Cross of Christ in worship, thanksgiving, and praise. Prayer prepares our hearts and minds for those things in front of us! Jesus prayed with all of His heart as He went to the cross. No longer can we afford to separate the heart from the cross. Just as the only sacrifice acceptable to God was the blood sacrifice of His perfect Son, the only heart that is acceptable to God is a *perfect heart* (1 Kgs. 8:61, Matt. 5:48 and 2 Tim. 3:17). Imperfection is no longer acceptable because all things of God and spiritual life from the cross are perfect (pure, complete, excellent, flawless and immaculate). Imperfection can never be one with perfection. A saved heart and life are operated by God's perfect love, the perfect blood of Jesus, His perfect word, peace, will and ways, perfect faith, and perfect salvation, wherein we look to go to that perfect place called Heaven.

Note: A perfect heart may also be interchangeable at times with a perfect spirit, our hidden man of the heart (1 Pet. 3:4).

The expository working of the *Heart of the Cross* renders every born again believer spiritually perfect in heart in God's sight, having been cleansed (washed) by the blood of the cross (Is. 1:18 and Rev. 1:5), by the cleansing and washing of the Word of God (Jn. 15:3) and of faith by God Himself (Acts 15:8-9). For years I was a member of the "Ain't nobody perfect" group, until I read Hebrews 10:14, which says: "For my one offering (Christ on Calvary) he has perfected forever them that are sanctified"! Because all Christian principles of life are heart-operated and cross-validated, we guard our perfect hearts that speak to God (Ps. 27:8), that may walk after the eyes (Job 31:7) after other evil hearts (Eze. 11:19-21), be deceitful above all things (Jer. 17:9-10), and yet seek after God (Jer. 29:11-13). The mind within us is our responsive system according to our nature and conscience. It holds our memories and reasoning factors, governs our thinking (thought life), mental capacity, imagination, comprehension, judgment, understanding, and intellect. It is renewed daily by the contents of our heart.

Being spiritually connected and infused, the mind and heart determine what our eyes see, how our ears hear, what our mouths speak, our Sunday service, seed, tithing, passion, sexuality, and are the base roots of our affections, compassions, and the operative genius of our will and emotions. Yet in spiritual matters we must never allow our minds to write checks that our hearts cannot cash. The heart may also be likened unto a great computer hard drive, the engine of an automobile, the sub-flooring of a great house, and a good fertile ground for the spiritual seeds we sow (Lk. 8:15). Far too many believers go to church on Sunday and fail to take their hearts with them. While church leaders are busy counting bodies, the Lord is counting hearts, especially those who belong to Him. We must keep our hearts in God's hands with a "whole heart" (all heart) concept, knowing our hearts are the only power on earth that can contain God, discern His will and walk with Him. The heart has the power to travel at the speed of thought. It also determines whether the seats (pews) of the church are full or empty on Sunday.

As we focus upon the *Heart of the Cross*, it may also be said that on Calvary man was at his worst, but God was at His best. Jesus was made sin for us (2 Cor. 5:21), He was made a curse for us (Gal. 3:13), all our sins and iniquities were put on Him by God the Father (Tit. 2:14). As our substitute (replacement, exchange), He died on Calvary in our place. We were guilty but He was innocent. I cross my heart. *The Heart of the Cross* has made us free (unchained, released,

Introduction: I Cross My Heart

liberated, and delivered) most assuredly (indeed, in fact, certainly, for sure, without question) (Jn. 8:31-36 and Gal. 5:1).

Here are some various types of crosses that were used for crucifixions during the time of Jesus Christ.*

As promised by God, we have a new free heart and a new spirit. Hebrews 12:1-2 instructs us in what we must do and why.

Wherefore, seeing we also are compressed about with so great a cloud of witness, let us lay aside every weight, and the sin which doth so easily beset us, and let us run with patience the race that is set before us, looking unto Jesus, the author and finisher of our faith, who for the joy that was set before him ENDURED THE CROSS, despising the shame, and is set down at the right hand of the throne of God.

I cross my heart that He came into our lives that we may come into His life. He first loved us that we may love Him and be like Him, even His brothers and sisters (Matt. 12:46-50). He is a friend to the friendless and upon the cross He was/is our friend indeed (Pr. 18:24, Jms. 2:23 and Jn. 15:13-15). Through the *Heart of the Cross* we become a vital part of who He is in the earth and He becomes the most precious part of who we are. Daily, we enjoy the great benefits of He, Him, and His, having a better understanding of I, me, my, and mine.

Yet there is much more to be revealed in this book. Above the mighty Cross of Jesus Christ, its significance and intrinsic value, stands the heart of God. Above our cross stands the loving, kind, forgiving, and awesome heart of Jesus Christ. Above the heart of every lost sinner stands the all-powerful, saving, and merciful heart of the Holy Spirit, at work drawing all unto salvation by grace through faith. *I cross my heart.*

Christ was cross-ordained from the foundation of this world as the slain Lamb of God (1 Pet. 1:18-20 and Rev. 13:8). God knows all His works toward mankind from the beginning of this world, and through Christ they were all completed (Acts 15:18 and Heb. 4:3).

In this book we shall view the three crosses that determine the works and end results of both natural and spiritual life.

1. The Cross of Jesus Christ (1 Cor. 1:17, Phil. 3:18 and Heb. 12:2)'
2. Our cross to bear (Matt. 6:24, 10:38 and Lk. 9:23)
3. The cross of the two thieves (Matt 27:44 and Mk. 15:27)

At Calvary, the people looked upon the Lord's face and I believe He looked upon their faces also. So often, facial expressions reveal our mindset, even the thoughts and emotions of our hearts.

*Artwork taken from the Webster's New World College Dictionary, page 330. Published by Houghton Mifflin Harcourt, Boston, 2014.

Chapter 1
A Look Upon My Face

"And it came to pass, when the time came that He should be received up (unto death on His cross for our sin salvation and redemption) *He steadfastly set His **face** to go to Jerusalem, and sent messengers before His **face**: and they went, and entered into a village of the Samaritans, to make ready for Him. And they did not receive Him, because His face was as though He would go to Jerusalem."* (Lk. 9:51-53) Jesus set His face to Calvary, to Golgotha (Jn. 19:16-18), the place of the skull, where they crucified Him outside of Jerusalem. His set face was a sure sign of a set heart and a ready mind, that would lead to the *Heart of the Cross*. Not only did the onlookers fail to discern His heart, but also the expression upon His beaten, bruised, and bloody face as they nailed Him to the cross.

His set face (look, appearance, expression) was also a good example of how our own faces as believers should be firmly set to prayer, to God's word with obedience, and to our cross, as we go forth to do God's will and works and follow Him. We must never allow our faces to become negatively (wrongly) impacted by wrong motives, ungodly emotions, heart grief, and pain. Otherwise it may take years before our hearts, minds, and God's grace are able to reset and restore our faces unto godliness, joy and peace, pleasing God and our loved ones. We must keep a positive look and an attitude of faith, such as "I will," "I am," "I can," and "I shall." These must always be graven upon our faces, for they are a sure defense against the powers of a worried look, a fearful or angry face, disappointment, and hopelessness, wherein we need a spiritual facelift. The only facelift believers should ever need is a face lifted unto God, as they look upon the *Heart of the Cross*. As we set our minds, hearts, and faces to run this race, we must focus (take heed, attend to) on our purpose and the call of God, knowing that because He lives we can face (view, endure, bear, and handle) tomorrow, and no weapon formed against us shall prosper. A set face unto the cross must be our top priority. It gives us strength to do, go, be, obey, and resist the devil. I have found that keeping a sound, renewed mindset and a pure and clean heartset, coupled with a daily diet of God's word, prayer, and worship, are excellent things to settle and keep our faces properly set.

Various dictionaries define the word *face* to mean appearance, visage, features, countenance, image, look, and expression. No doubt the Lord on Calvary had the face of a great loving, caring, forgiving, and passionate *Shepherd of Israel* (Ps. 80:1). (See Gen. 49:24 and Ps. 12:1) He looked upon them with the merciful face of a true and loving friend, even of publicans (tax collectors) and sinners (Matt. 11:19 and Jn. 15:12-15); the friendly face that *sticks closer than a brother* (Pr. 17:17 and 18:24). On this day, among the onlookers, ignorance ruled supreme, stupidity rejoiced, and imbecility rested upon almost every face, mind, heart, and soul. Again I say, not only did the people not discern His heart (who He really was), they failed to discern the look of love upon His face. Let us not forget how Jesus Christ, as He was on His way to Calvary, fell down upon His face and prayed unto His Father, saying: "*Oh, my Father, if it be possible, let this cup pass from me; nevertheless, not as I will but as you will.*" (Matt 26:39-42).

In Genesis 17:1-8, God appeared unto Abraham, making a serious covenant with him that would affect this whole world. Though Abraham was ninety-nine years old, God spoke to him, saying that Sarah, his wife, would bear a son and he would become the father of many nations. Abraham <u>fell on his face and God talked with him there</u>. In Luke 5:12-13, a leper fell on his face before Jesus and was healed. (See Lk. 17:12-19) In 2 Kings 20:2, King Hezekiah was sick unto death. He turned his <u>face</u> to the wall and prayed unto the Lord with a perfect heart, and God added fifteen years to his life.

Falling upon our faces daily before God in prayer may be a deeper anointed way of worship and prayer than folded hands, lifted arms, or bowed knees alone, giving honor, thanksgiving and glory unto God. Just as we can have a double heart, there may also be a double face. On Sunday, a holy face that looks clean and outwardly beautiful in truth can be as a mask; deceptive, false, even a lie. The Lord, through His cross, not only has given us eternal life, but by His peace and joy a wrinkle-free and frown-free face, showing forth His likeness, glory, and image (Rom. 8:29 and Col. 3:10). (See Gen. 1:26-27)

In Psalm 17:15, David beheld God's face in righteousness. In Genesis 32:30, Jacob beheld God face-to-face. In Exodus 33:11, God spoke to Moses face-to-face. In 2 Chronicles 7:14, we are commanded to humble ourselves, pray, and *seek God's face*, and He will forgive our sins and heal our land. God has a face our hearts should seek daily. *"When you said seek my face, my heart said unto thee, thy face, Lord, will I seek."* David continues, saying: *"Hide not thy face far from me: put not thy servant away in anger"* (Ps 27:8-9). The Prophet Isaiah shed some light upon this issue, saying: *"But your iniquities have separated between you and your God, and your sins have <u>hidden His face from you</u>, and He will not hear. Your hands are defiled with blood, and your fingers with iniquity; your lips have spoken lies, and your tongue hath muttered perverseness."* (Is. 59:1-3) (See Ps. 104:29) We must keep in mind that the contents of our hearts operated all the above, especially our facial countenance, expressions, and intentions. We can rest assured that by His grace we can enjoy a holy face if we allow Jesus Christ to dwell in our most holy place called the heart.

As the Lord hung upon His cross, not only did they spit in His face (Matt. 26:67), but His visage (facial appearance, features, profile, countenance, look) was marred (destroyed, ruined, devastated) more than any man, and His form (figure, body) more than the sons of any man (Is. 52:14 and Lk. 22:64-65). His facial features were no longer in human form, but a bloody display, a horrible countenance, beaten and torn more terribly than any face ever recorded or ever would be recorded upon the earth. Yet on the third day He rose from the grave, having a new face and new body, clean, holy, perfect, and godly. By this, our faces could represent His face, and from our hearts we could give light and knowledge of the glory of God in the face of Jesus Christ (2 Cor. 4:3-6). We could be like Him in His image. There is an emergency need for believers to receive the gift of discernment of hearts and of faces, for there are many false faces, evil countenances and wicked expressions among us.

I had a dear friend who owned his own Bible store. One day I asked him to give me every picture of Jesus he had in the store. He brought me seven, and all of them were not the same. Beware! This is symbolism, typology, and a metaphor at its very worst (out of order) presentation. Needless to say, we were both amazed (surprised, astonished). It is very evident that too many biblical leaders and religions have failed to discern the Lord's face, mind, and heart. This is very serious, for most of those who are still alive upon the earth at the very end will not recognize Him when He comes. I have noticed how rich wives, ladies of the evening, famous singers, and successful business people spend hundreds of dollars per month seeking to keep their faces beautiful (lovely, clean, and attractive).

Yet without being saved and given a new heart and a godly face, they soon become bound in life with one or more of these faces:
- A sad, sorrowful face (Neh. 2:1-3, Job 16:16, and Matt. 6:16)
- An angry, fearful and hard face (Pr. 21:29)
- An impudent (shameless, rude, and lustful) face (Pr. 7:13)
- A sinful, depressed, unhappy, and shameful face (Ps. 69:6-7, 83:16-18, Jer. 51:51 and Eze. 7:18)
- A pale face (Is. 29:22 and Jer. 30:6)

While we all love to enjoy a smiling face, let us not forget God's promise of the shining face of His countenance. *"The Lord will bless thee, and keep thee; the Lord will make His face shine upon thee, and be gracious unto thee; the Lord will lift up His countenance upon thee, and give thee peace"* (Num. 6:24-26). We must become like the great Psalmist David, who petitioned for God's face to shine upon him (Ps. 31:16 and 80:3). I encourage every leader to intently observe the faces of the people assigned to them, that there be no playboys in the pulpit, singing jezebels in choir, hypocrites or sex bandits leading in any auxiliary capacity. Satan is their god and most assuredly they shall see their god face-to-face, as we shall see our God.

The heart holds the keys as to which God we shall see and serve forever (Rev. 22:1-5). Jesus spoke of His Father's face (Matt. 18:10). Our blind eyes are now open (2 Kgs. 6:17 and Acts 26:18), our deaf ears are now open to hear His voice, and our mouths that once were closed are open wide to worship, pray, give thanks, and praise (2 Cor. 6:11, Ps. 34:15, 81:10 and 1 Pet. 3:12). There may not be anything more precious in God's presence than an open face, mind, and heart.

"But we all, with open face beholding as in a mirror (glass) *the glory of the Lord, are changed into the same image from glory to glory, by the Spirit of the Lord"* (2 Cor. 3:18). (See Jms. 1:23-24)

Facial Heart Expression

In the beginning, God created a garden in Eden. He created Adam and Eve and placed them in the garden. They were the beginning (origin) of human life, the ancestors of the whole human race upon the earth. Because the garden was a type of Heaven on Earth, Adam and Eve wore happy, smiling, peaceful, kind, clean, joyful, and lovely faces. In Genesis 2:16-17, God gave instructions for

Adam not to eat of the Tree of the Knowledge of Good and Evil. Satan with his ugly face entered into the garden and imparted into their hearts (nature and genetic codes) the sinful poison of disobedience and belief in a lie. They ate from the forbidden tree. This greatly pleased Satan. Because sin and rebellion (disobedience) changes the heart that governs our facial expressions, Adam and Eve's facial expressions now included worry, guilt, fear, sadness, sin, and shame. They became separated from God (Is. 59:2) and took upon themselves death and demonic facial expressions, such as lust, depression, ungodliness, disappointment, anger (Pr. 25:23), tears (Is. 25:8), impudence (Pr. 7:13), and confusion (Dan. 9:7-8). Not only was the sin issue given birth unto all mankind, but every soul born of a woman would now be subjected to Satan's negative facial expressions.

Adam and Eve heard the voice of the Lord God walking in the garden in the cool of the day, and they hid themselves (their faces) from the presence (face) of the Lord God among the trees of the garden (Gen. 3:8). God excommunicated (banished, removed, dismissed) them from the garden. They gave birth unto two sons, Cain and Abel. Cain was continually angry with his brother, because Abel's offering pleased God. Daily Cain's countenance (visage, face, look, appearance, expression) was fallen (immoral, wicked). The Lord said unto Cain: *"Why are you angry, and why is your countenance fallen?"* When Cain killed his brother, Abel, he became cursed, punished, and lived in fear. While God looks upon the heart, we can see He also views the countenance and expressions of our faces, how they are directly heart-connected. Habitually we listen to the words of our mouths and fail to discern what our facial expressions are saying. A facial expression is an outward showing and display of our inward emotions, heart opinions, desires, feelings, beliefs, mindset, thoughts, and imagination. They have the power to speak for hours or many days without words, such as with a smile, pout, grimace, contortion, frown, downcast countenance, or an open display of anger or fear.

The state, condition, and contents of our hearts are the key factors. They are no less than the results of our hearts speaking and expressing their will, desires, concerns, dislikes, or pleasure without words. Facial heart expressions are open responses to an issue, problem or blessing. While our mouth expression means to put into words, vocalize, articulate, communicate, say or speak, the facial expression is a look, appearance, countenance, the casting and exposition of our facial character. In plain sight, the heart is well able to hide many things. This is because it has the ability to see with the eyes, hear with the ears, and express itself through the mouth while showing its true feelings, desires, will and emotions only through an expression. For this it is imperative (extremely requested) that we be well able to discern and read the facial expressions of others, especially our own. A clean heart and a right mind will always work for the better and right facial expressions. We must be wise, beware, and be on guard of what we hear, see, say, and do, because our hearts are well able to express their own opinions, ideas, beliefs, and plans upon our faces. Facial expressions begin in our lives from the crib, and will show themselves until we go to our heavenly home.

I shall never forget the time I went to a friend's house to see and pray for their young child, about four months old. The mother gave him into my arms to hold and pray. He had been such a happy young lad until I held in him in my arms. Immediately his facial expression changed into shock, dismay, and disbelief. He began to yell and scream as loudly as he could, squinting his face, kicking his feet, and flailing his little arms until I quickly returned him to his mother. Then all was well.

A blank (expressionless, impassive, vague, inscrutable, barren) face may well be the most dangerous facial expression of all. It has the power to give God lip service on Sunday, yet on Monday the hearts of such people are far from God (Mk. 7:5-8). A blank face is often found upon a thief, hypocrite, pretender, or child molester, being governed by an evil, deceitful heart. Only God really knows their true intentions and the actual condition of their minds and hearts. Some who are expressionless and heartless are also blank to the point of being faceless. Therefore, the best time to observe the facial expressions of people is during prayer, worship, and praise, as the Word goes forth in God's presence. God's presence is well able to cause a true expression to rest upon a blank face. Facial expressions may begin to appear long before there is a change of character, personality, nature, attitude, mindset, or behavior. None should trust a speaking tongue (mouth or lips) if their expressions are not in harmony with the right words being spoken. Just as the heart is the first organ to be fully functional within us, it is also the first to express its will, plans, and desires upon our faces. This is because facial expressions are most certainly heart-ruled and mind-connected. A heart attack or a negative emotional response from the heart will often cause a negative facial look, a contortion, a cast down appearance, even the face becoming sad and fallen. Some **negative** facial expressions are: shock, worry, hate, fear, anger, grief (sadness, sorrow), and disappointment (failed expectations). Some positive facial expressions are: joy, gladness, peace, laughter, happiness, satisfaction (being pleased), unexpected blessings, and good (legal) sex. Some of the facial expressions we see are no less than deep heart expressions we do not see. For this we observe the eyes that are direct pathways to and from the heart, such as an evil eye (Mk. 7:22), lying eyes (Pr. 23:6), tear-stained eyes (Job 16:20), or blind eyes (Mt. 20:33-34, Jn. 12:40); keeping in mind how the eyes seriously affect the heart (Lam. 3:51). Little have we considered that some of our facial expressions in God's presence may be offensive to Him. On Calvary, the day of the execution of our Lord and Savior Jesus Christ, there were many negative heart expressions upon the faces of the people. These expressions were also formed because of sin, hate, disobedience, and the rejection of Jesus Christ as their Lord and Savior.

The answer to wrong expressions is to ask God for a right heart so our facial countenance will also be right before both God and man.

The Cross of the Two Thieves

There were also two others, malefactors, led with Christ to be put to death. When they came to the place called Calvary, there they crucified Him, and the malefactors (criminals, convicts, evildoers, villains, outlaws, murderers and sinners); one on the right hand and the other on the left (Lk. 23:32-34). Like Jesus, the two thieves carried a cross the people could see and also a spiritual cross that could not be seen. Their spiritual cross of evil, wrongdoing and wickedness caused them to be in the

precarious position they were in. Most importantly, let us take notice of the hearts of the two thieves, which represent the heart types of every lost sinner on earth. The natural cross they carried was made by the hands of men, but their spiritual cross by the corrupt and wicked hands of Satan, who spends most of his time drawing, deceiving, and propelling lost hearts of all sinners into his ungodly kingdom, regardless (irrespective) of age or ethnic background.

No doubt their hearts were foolish (Pr. 15:7, 12:23), dark (Rom. 1:21), blind (Eph. 4:18), lost, sin-filled, and defiled (unclean, corrupt, and dirty). Beaten, bruised, in pain, and suffering, the two thieves carried their crosses to Calvary, not failing to see that their own hearts, minds, and evil works had brought them to the threshold of death and eternal condemnation. In Mark 7:21-23, Jesus revealed this: *"For from within, out of the heart of men proceed evil thoughts, adulteries, fornication, murders, theft, covetousness, wickedness, deceit, lasciviousness* (lust, sensual, fleshly carnality), *an evil eye, blasphemy* (cursing, lewdness, sacrilege), *pride, foolishness. All these evil things come from within and defile a man."* (See Matt. 6:19-21 and 21:13, Rev. 9:20-21). As the people stood looking at the bruised, bloody and beaten bodies of the two thieves, the beguiling factors were that few (if any) who stood by were cognizant of the true state (condition) of their own hearts, the hearts of the two thieves, or the pure, clean and loving heart of their Lord and Savior Jesus Christ. This is because heart illiteracy was worldwide then, like it still is today.

The heart that governs and rules the lifestyle of a thief is also a lying heart. One that is cold, wicked, deceptive, lost, and loves to steal, kill and destroy, especially in secret. A thief is also listed as a robber, burglar, a pickpocket, bandit, shoplifter, holdup man, criminal, embezzler, and a thug. In John 10:1 and 10, the Lord warns us that the thief comes not but to steal, kill and to destroy; meaning that if anyone comes to God other than the way of the Cross and true repentance, the same is a thief and a robber. We must conclude that the two thieves in their hearts were outlaws, con-men, swindlers, rapists, cheaters, looters, and murderers under Satan's power. They were worthy of death, Hell, and the grave, the same as most of those who were standing by. Many of the onlookers were already as if dead in their trespasses and sins (Rom. 5:12, 2 Cor. 5:21, and Gal. 3:22). In 1 Corinthians 6:9-22, the Apostle Paul revealed to us that before we were saved, born again, sanctified, justified, and made righteous, and washed and redeemed by the blood of the Cross, as lost sinners, spiritually we were the same as the two thieves (Gal. 5:16-20). We were children of Satan in our hearts, works, conversations, and spirits (Jn. 8:44 and 1 Jn. 3:8-10). Because both the saved and lost have a cross to bear, Satan rejoices when a lost sinner perishes upon the cross of sin and death he has evilly provided for them. Let us not forget that in Heaven, Satan was perfect, but when his heart became lifted up because of pride and his beauty, he was cast out and down to the ground. (Eze. 28:1-19). In Isaiah 14:12-14, the Prophet Isaiah gives us the allegory (story) of his fall:

"*How art thou cut down to the ground, who did weaken the nations! For thou has <u>said in thine heart</u>, I will ascend into heaven, I will exalt my throne above the stars of God; I will sit upon the mount of the congregation, in the sides of the north, I will ascend above the heights of the clouds, I will be like the most high.*" Being cast down to earth, he came to the Garden of Eden and caused Adam and Eve to obey him. He became the god of this world, having many types of evil devices with which to deceive and defile all mankind. Some types can be seen within the two thieves who hung on their crosses at Calvary with Jesus Christ. They had made a great mistake in life, in that they never gave their hearts to God to serve Him and keep His commandments. Yet, one of the thieves found favor with God, saying: "*Lord, when you come into your Kingdom, remember me.*" He now believed in his heart that Jesus Christa was his Lord and Savior. Jesus replied: "*Verily, verily, I say unto thee, today shall thou be with me in paradise.*" (Lk. 23:43). As death came forth upon them, Christ spoke to Satan, saying: "*This is your hour and the power of darkness*" (Lk. 22:53). Revelation reveals that God has a plan that was simply awesome. In death, Satan's type of hearts filled all three crosses. For a moment, Satan rejoiced. When Jesus revived and rose the third day in victory, all evil types of hearts of Satan were defeated, and the good hearts of God were restored and given to all who would repent and believe. Here are some of the types of hearts of Satan that could be seen upon the Cross at Calvary.

Some Heart Types of Satan and the Two Thieves on Calvary

	Hard: John 12:40, Romans 2:5 and Hebrews 3:8 **Adulterous:** Matthew 5:28 and Mark 7:21 **Evil:** Hebrews 3:12, Genesis 6:5 and Jeremiah 7:24 **Blind:** Ephesians 4:18 and 2 Corinthians 3:14	
Doubting: Mark 11:23 and Luke 12:19 **Sinful & Sick:** Proverbs 13:12, Isaiah 1:5 and 2 Corinthians 5:21 **Deceitful:** Jeremiah 17:9-10, 23:26, Isaiah 44:20 and Proverbs 12:10	**Lost:** Mark 7:6-9 and 1 John 3:20-21 **Unbelief:** Hebrews 3:12 and Revelation 21:8 **Error:** 2 Timothy 2:18, 1 John 4:6 and Hebrews 3:10	**Disobedient:** Ephesians 2:2, 5:6, Colossians 3:6 and Titus 1:16 **Foolish:** Psalm 53:1, Romans 1:2-11, Proverbs 8:5 and 12:23 **Thief:** Matthew 15:19 and 1 Corinthians 6:10
	Uncircumcised: Leviticus 26:41, Jeremiah 9:26 and Ezekiel 44:7-9 **Unclean:** Isaiah 64:6 and Galatians 5:19 **Proud:** Psalm 101:5, Proverbs 16:18 and 1 John 2:16	

Because the two thieves were Satan's slaves and representatives, their hearts gave presentation for all the above types of hearts on the earth. In addition to these, there are other types of hearts used by Satan that I call *The Terrible Un-Family of Hearts* that make war against God's heavenly heart family, the Cross of Christ and *God's Mighty Kingdom of Hearts*. The strength and power of the un-family of hearts lie in the fact that they are interchangeable with most of the hearts represented by the two thieves on Calvary.

- Unstable heart (Is. 21:4, Jms. 1:8, 2 Pet. 2:14 and 3:16)
- Unholy heart (Lev. 10:10, 1 Tim. 1:9, and 2 Tim. 3:2)
- Unclean heart (Is. 64:6, Gal. 5:19)
- Unperfect heart (1 Kgs. 11:4, 15:3, and 2 Chron. 25:2)
- Unwise heart (Is. 21:4, Jms. 1:8, 2 Pet. 2:14 and 3:16)
- Unfaithful heart (Pr. 25:19)
- Ungodly heart (2 Sam. 22:5, Ps. 1:1-6, Rom. 5:6, 2 Tim. 2:16 and Tit. 2:12)
- Uncircumcised heart (Lev. 26:41, Jer. 9:26, Eze. 44:7-9)
- Unruly heart (1 Thess. 5:14, Tit. 1:10, and Jms. 3:8)
- Unthankful heart (Lk. 6:35 and 2 Tim. 3:2)
- Unbelieving heart (Mk. 16:14 and Heb. 3:12)
- Unloyal heart (1 Kgs. 11:4, 15:3, and 2 Chron. 25:2)

Because our God is ever-present to give unto every one of us the type of heart we need for victory and glory, here are several things we can ask Him for:
1. A new heart (Eze. 11:19-21, 36:26, Heb. 10:16)
2. A clean (blood-washed) heart (Jer. 4:14, Ps. 51:10, Jn. 15:3, Rev. 1:5)
3. A renewed and changed mind (1 Sam. 2:35, Rom. 12:2, Phil. 4:7, Jms. 4:8)
4. A prepared heart (Pr. 16:1 and 1 Chron. 29:18)
5. An established heart (1 Thess. 3:13 and Jms. 5:8)
6. A fixed heart (Ps. 57:7 and 112:1)
7. A wise heart (1 Kgs. 3:12, Pr. 8:33 and 10:8), and a right mind (1 Chron. 28:9 and 2 Pet. 3:1)

This is so very important. Let us look closer at the condemnation of the two thieves. In Philippians 3:18-19, we read that *"many walk, of whom I have told you often, and now tell you even weeping, that they are <u>The Enemies of The Cross of Christ</u>, whose end is destruction, whose God is their appetite* (belly) *and whose glory is in their shame; whose mind is set on earthly things."* As I said before, the two thieves had sinned and made terrible mistakes in life, so they never gave their hearts and lives to God, to serve and obey Him, keeping His laws, word, and commandments, which is the greatest mistake of all. One of the crucified malefactors railed at Jesus (talked angrily, screamed with rage and shouted), saying: *"If thou be the Christ* (anointed one) *save* *thyself and us. But the other answering rebuked him saying, don't you fear God, seeing that you are in the same condemnation? And we indeed, justly; for we receive the due reward of our deeds. But this man* (Christ) *hath done nothing amiss. And he said unto Jesus, Lord, remember me when you come unto your Kingdom. And Jesus said unto him* (from the Heart of the Cross), *Verily I say unto thee, today shalt though be with me in paradise!"* (Lk. 23:39-43) (See also Matt. 27:38-44, Mk. 15:24-32, Jn. 10:8 and 1 Cor. 6:9-11)

No doubt this one thief was the wiser of the two. His saying from his heart caused him to find favor with God. His blind eyes were now opened. He had a change of mind and heart. He now believed in his heart that Jesus Christ was Lord. He received Him as Lord and Savior and was saved. By revelation, he crossed over from eternal death unto eternal life, casting aside the evil cross of Satan and his unclean kingdom of hearts. This is proof and truth that will stand forever that *God is greater than our hearts,* regardless of whatever type they may be. For if our hearts condemn us, *"God is greater than our heart, and He knows all things. Beloved if our heart condemns us not, then we have confidence* (faith, trust, assurance) *towards God."* (1 Jn. 3:20-21)

God's heart is greater than all hearts. It is full of love, grace, and mercy unto every thief and is salvation for every lost soul, no matter what type of negative heart they may have. Yet to be saved (born again), all must come to *The Heart of the Cross.*

Lift Him Up

In John 12:32-33, the Lord spoke to the people, saying: *"and I, if I be lifted up from the earth I will draw all men unto me."* Now that the beatings, shame, pulling out the hair of His beard, and nailing His hands and feet to the cross were completed, evil-hearted men took hold of the cross and lifted Him up. Again referring to **Webster's New World Dictionary**, it defines the word *lift* (lifted, lifting) to mean to raise up, elevate, pick up, hoist or uplift. The Lord's promise when He was lifted up to draw all men unto Himself is a great promise of the heart that still stands today. He draws our hearts unto Him. While they were lifting Him up for evil, it was working for our good. Even to this day, the more we lift Him, the more He draws (pulls, lures, drags, evokes) the hearts of mankind unto Himself.

That dreadful day as they lifted up the Lord on Calvary, they were ignorant of the fact that they were lifting up God's own heart, body, mind, and soul, the Creator, the Word, the Lamb of God, the Son of God, our Savior, Redeemer, Messiah, Lord, King of Kings, and God manifest in human form, just to name a few. Most certainly for the first and last time, the Lord's heart was in the hands of men. Because we were spiritually in Christ (Jn. 14:20, 15:3-7, and 2 Cor. 5:17), even during His death, burial, and resurrection (Rom. 6:3-10, Col. 2:12 and 20), we are/were risen with Him (Col. 3:1). The lifting of Christ was threefold:

1. Lifting Him up on Calvary (Jn. 3:14 and 8:28)
2. Lifting Him up from the grave (Rom. 8:11)
3. Lifting Him up from the earth unto Heaven and glory (Mk. 16:19 and Acts 1:2-22)

If evil men can lift Him up for evil, how much more should we, as His people, lift Him up for our good? Because our lifting is from our hearts, we lift Him up with our voices, with our hands, singing, praises, worship, thanksgiving, and lifestyle. In every church sanctuary as cross believers, we lift Him up individually and collectively with all our hearts. Yet we must remember the goodness of God, who lifts us up as He is lifted. *"Humble yourselves in the sight of the Lord, and He shall lift you up"* (Jms. 4:10).

"I would, therefore, that men pray everywhere, lifting up holy hands, without wrath and doubting" (1 Tim. 2:8). We can clearly see that for us to lift up holy hands, we must be holy (godly, virtuous, moral, pure, clean), having a holy spirit and heart within us. Lamentations 3:41 instructs us to lift up our hearts with our hands unto God in the Heavens. In the midst of our praises and worship, we (by faith) take hold of our spiritual hearts and all they contain and lift them up unto the Lord. This will enhance our love for God (Mk. 12:28-33), our faith in God (Rom. 10:10-11), as we walk in obedience to God's will, word, and voice with our whole hearts (Rom. 6:17). To avoid having many church services without God's presence, we lift up His great name as we come boldly unto His throne of grace. David wrote in Psalm 25:1, saying: *"unto thee, O Lord, do I lift up my soul;"* and in Psalm 28:9, he asked God to save His people, to bless them, feed them, and to lift them up forever. Being a lifter of God, he made a vow unto the Lord, saying: *"I will lift up mine eyes unto the hills. From whence cometh my help?"* (Ps. 121:1) (See also Ps. 3:3 and 40:2). As we humble ourselves before the *Heart of the Cross*, we lift up our loved ones before God, those who are in leadership and presidential authority. We must be

extremely careful not to lift up ourselves with pride. We guard our hearts, keeping in remembrance Satan who became lifted up in his heart and was cast out of Heaven (Is. 14:12-14 and Eze. 28:1-6). (See also Deut. 8:14-19).

Chapter 2
The Heart Of The Cross

God has a great heart. He is all heart. He operates all life forms by the contents and desires of His very own heart, having knowledge of all things in Heaven and Earth by His infinite and unlimited mind. In the beginning of creation, out of God's heart (bosom) and mouth came forth the Word of God, saying: "*Let there be light,*" and there was light (Gen. 1:3, Heb. 11:3). The *Word of God* went forth creating all things as "God The Word," (Jn. 1:1-3 and 14) which was no less than God at work in all of creation. There came a season, due to the fall of Adam and Eve, when God saw that the thoughts (perceptions, mental activity, knowing, mediations) and the imaginations (visualized pictures, visions, insight, mind's eye, inventions) of men were continually evil and it <u>grieved Him</u> in His heart. He spoke the Word, and the Word brought forth a great flood upon the whole earth. This great Word of God came down through forty-two generations, went into Mary's womb, created a Human body for Himself and came forth into the earth as Jesus Christ, God's Son, the Word, the Lamb of God, who was both God and man in a body, according to the scriptures (Is. 9:6, 1 Tim. 3:16 and Tit. 2:9-14). Jesus the Christ, the Living Word, who had made all things as God the Word, had become flesh and now dwelled among men.

"*In the beginning was the <u>Word</u>, and the <u>Word</u> was with God, and the <u>Word</u> was God. The same was in the beginning with God. All things were by Him; and without Him was not anything made that was made*" (Jn. 1:1-3) In verse 14: "*and the <u>Word</u> was made flesh, and dwelt among us and we beheld His glory as of the only begotten of the Father, full of grace and truth.*" (See also Col. 1:16, Heb. 11:3, 1 Jn. 5:7 and Rev. 19:13). As the Lamb of God, our Savior, Lord, God the Word and Redeemer, He was also <u>God's Heart</u> at work in the Earth to manifest and bring to fruition *The Heart of the Cross*, as only He could. Because all living beings live and function by the operation of their hearts, we must conclude that the Heart of the Trinity (Godhead) is also *The Heart of the Cross*, wherein lies the light of life for all humanity, to include salvation, forgiveness of sins, love, redemption, prayer, our belief, eternal life, faith, hope, and the grace of God fulfilling the *Heart of the Cross* of Jesus Christ.

Even though Jesus as Christ was first mentioned in the New Testament book of Matthew, He was identified in the Old Testament (Is. 9:6 and 53:1-12) as God's sinless Son, the Anointed One, the Lord, Messiah, God's voice, Branch of Righteousness, and especially as the Lamb of God that was slain from the foundation of the world. *"And all that dwell upon the earth shall worship him* (the antichrist) *whose names are not written in the Lamb's book of life of the <u>Lamb slain from the foundation of the world</u>"* (Jn. 1:29, Rev. 13:8 and 20:12-15). This indicates that the Cross of Christ is/was authentic, was set up, and finished by God the Father from the very beginning of creation. Christ would be the power and glory of it, our victory, life giver, blood donor, sacrifice replacement and blesser. All that Jesus Christ did on earth was to complete and fulfill what His Father had already carefully planned and completed in Heaven and in His heart from the beginning for the benefit of all mankind.

The real issue began with Satan in Heaven before creation began. Satan had evilly created within himself a spirit of rebelliousness, greed, and other types of hearts contrary to God's will and plans. Deadly and powerful hearts such as lying, evil, lustful, deceitful, disobedient, and defiled (corrupt, polluted, contaminated, dirty) hearts. Isaiah 14:12-14 reveals it came to pass that Satan said these words in his dark, sinful, proud, and wicked heart. *"<u>I will</u> exalt my throne above the stars of God: <u>I will</u> sit also upon the mount of the congregation in the sides of the North, <u>I will</u> ascend above the heights of the clouds, <u>I will</u> be like The Most High."* He was ignorant of the fact that God hears what our hearts are saying without words being audibly spoken. He listens to the voice of our hearts. Satan's desire was to set up his own kingdom of hearts to rule as god over God's Kingdom of Hearts. God expelled him and his angels out of His presence in Heaven. He became the father and creator of all sin, sickness, lies, disease, death; the author of nothing, King of Not, and ruler of Never Will Be (Rev. 12:7-12). (See also Eze. 28:1-7) Satan is the deceiver of hearts.

Heart deception is one of the worst kinds of all. He came into the Garden of Eden, deceived the heart of Eve, who would give birth unto sin and all ungodliness by Adam, her husband. Satan was pleased and stood as the god of this world, the supreme ruler, and power of darkness (2 Cor. 4:3-6). Yet God had a plan filled with His divine purpose. Known unto God are all His works from the beginning of the world (Acts 15:18). He sent His only begotten Son from the beginning (Rev. 13:8) to destroy the works of the devil. *"He that committeth sin is of the devil; for the devil sinneth from the beginning. For this purpose the Son of God was manifested that He might destroy the works of the devil."* (1 Jn. 3:8) The only way Satan could be defeated forever would be by the crucifixion, death, burial, and resurrection of Jesus Christ, who would die on Calvary as the Lamb of God, but would rise up on the third day as our Alpha and Omega, our Lord of Lords, the Lion of Judah, the Messiah, our Savior, and King of Kings.

After the Lord's Supper (Matt. 26:26-29), Satan entered into Judas Iscariot, one of the twelve. He went his way and communed (conferred) with the chief priests and captains how he might betray Him (Jesus) unto them. (Lk. 22:3). They were glad and covenanted to give him money. John, the Lord's bosom disciple, writes in John 13:23-30 that after eating of the Passover, *Satan entered into Judas and then said Jesus unto him, what thou doest do quickly.* I believe that Satan entered into the heart of Judas Iscariot. Not only is he a heart thief, but also a *heart molester*, loving to vex, trouble, terrify, and abuse every heart on Earth. He seeks to infiltrate, invade, penetrate, impregnate, and impact our hearts without our permission. For our defense, our hearts must be filled with the <u>Seed Word of God</u>. In Luke 8:12, the devil comes to take the written word out of their hearts, lest they should believe and be saved. (See Jn. 10:10 and Jms. 4:7) Judas Iscariot failed to recognize that Satan, the lord of all sin, sickness and disease, ruler of death, hell and the grave, the liar, deceiver, unclean beast, the illegal god of this world, had enticed him to betray God's only Son for thirty pieces of silver.

"And they took Jesus, and led Him away. And He, bearing His cross, went forth into a place called the "place of a skull," which is called in the Hebrew, Golgotha, where they crucified Him, and two others with Him (one on each side) *and Jesus was in the center* (midst). *And Pilate wrote a title, and put it on the cross. And the writing was, Jesus of Nazareth, King of the Jews."* (Jn. 19:16-22 and Lk. 23:33-38) It was customary for the sin(s) of the guilty person being crucified to be written upon their cross. What Pilate wrote about Jesus was not a sin, He was sinless; but one of the greatest infallible truths about Jesus Christ in the Bible. He was/is King of Kings, the King of Glory, the King of the Jews and Lord of Lords. Pilate wrote it in Greek, Latin, and Hebrew and when

the leaders tried to get him to change it, he refused (Jn. 19:19-22). It may well be he remembered the many works and miracles the Lord had done without sin. When the chief priests, captains of the temple, and the elders came out to arrest Him with swords and clubs, He spoke to their hearts as to Satan, saying; "*this is your hour and the power of darkness*" (Lk. 22:52-53).

In the last 2,000 years, thousands of books have been written about the Cross of Jesus Christ, His death, burial, and resurrection, and yet there is another vital part of this great story that must be revealed and it has been given unto me to write and reveal it. For hundreds of years, millions upon millions have looked upon the picture of Jesus Christ as He hung there between Heaven and hell upon His cross. They have looked upon His torn, bruised, and beaten body and have <u>failed to see His great, loving, and forgiving heart</u>, the *Heart of the Cross*! The great and matchless Heart of God! They knew His body, but not His heart and mind. When there is no knowledge of God's Heart, there is no true knowledge of Him. Who we really are is predicated upon the state, condition, and contents of our hearts. *To know God is to know His heart* (Jer. 24:7 and 2 Thess. 1:8). Ignorant men look, stare, and gaze upon the outward appearance, but God looks upon the heart (1 Sam. 16:7). He knows the heart (1 Kgs. 8:39 and Acts 1:24), which includes His own heart, our hearts, the heart of His Son, the hearts of all those who stood by crying out and shouting, "Crucify Him," unto those who put Him to death, and those who failed to detect His great heart. Like unto some of us, the religious leaders were so evilly focused upon their purpose, they failed to discern reality and truth. Heart detection is by far the most important thing. On Calvary, the Lord was heart-motivated, purposed, heart-prepared, and determined, being driven to the cross, beaten, bruised, scandalized (dishonored), humiliated (disgraced, embarrassed) and wounded more than any man ever was. Yet none considered His heart on Calvary, His thoughts, grief, desires, emotions, pain, and brokenness that existed within His bruised, broken, and blood-stained body.

Truly the Cross of Jesus was/is the greatest heart event that has ever taken place upon the earth, wherein God's only Son became our sin offering and sacrifice unto God for us all (Is. 53:10, Heb. 7:27, 9:11-28, 10:5-18 and 11:27). He <u>became</u> sin and a curse for us (Gal. 3:13). We must consider the hearts of those who spat on Him and dishonored Him to the maximum level of dishonor, shame, and total disrespect. The horrible beating and sufferings of Jesus Christ showed forth the wickedness of man's heart and the evilness of their sin-sick minds and souls. Yet in His heart Jesus loved them, forgave them and went forth unto death for the redemption and salvation of their souls. Though men saw the tears that fell from His eyes like great drops of blood (Lk. 22:44), they failed to discern the state His great tear-stained and crying heart that contained His blood, breath (air), and life (water). They didn't know His heart was a blood pump, air, life, and water pump for the whole world. It wasn't the fear of the cross that caused great tears to flow from His eyes, but the knowledge He would be separated from His Father and the disciples He loved. We know tears from the heart speak words to God and man that are often beyond our ability to comprehend and articulate. It would please the professional killers of the cross whenever they would hear their victims scream in pain and suffering, crying and gasping for breath, and begging for mercy as they were being crucified. To their surprise, Jesus, as He was being crucified, never said a mumbling word as was expected. He never allowed His heart to speak. The mouth, likened unto a tear-stained face, often speaks and reveals the state, position, and condition of the heart. In His heart, He had nothing more to say. *The Heart of the Cross* was silent.

In John 10:17-18, Jesus confessed this about His cross, saying: *"Therefore doth my Father love me, because I lay down my life that I may take it again. No man taketh it from me, but I lay it down of myself. I have power to lay it down, and I have power to take it again."* (See also Jn. 14:31 and Heb. 10:5-14) No death could kill Him and no grave could hold Him. He hung suspended between Heaven and hell as guilty before man but innocent before God. With a loving heart He gave His life freely, He laid it down and then He willfully died (Mk. 15:37-39). Before Satan and his demonic angels could touch Him and claim the victory, Jesus stopped His own heart from beating. In reality, both His Father and disciples (except John and Mary) had departed from Him. He was heartbroken, shattered, naked, smashed into pieces, damaged, hurt, inoperative, literally disconnected and separated. It may well be said that the heart of Jesus was broken on Calvary so that our hearts may be mended and made whole in this life. Anyone who becomes brokenhearted is despondent, crushed, grieved, sad, inconsolable, dejected, and miserable, unable to function in life and their purpose as required. Jesus had come to heal the brokenhearted (Is. 61:1-3 and Lk. 4:18), but on Calvary's cross He chose not to heal

His own broken heart. The Lord in John 18:37 revealed this to Pontius Pilate, who disrespectfully interrogated Him: *"To this end was I born and for this cause I came into the world that I should bear witness unto the truth"* (See also 12:26-32).

It is by the *Heart of the Cross* we have continual revelation of the cross at Calvary (See 1 Tim. 3:16 and 1 Jn. 3:5-8). **Webster's Dictionary** further defines the word *Calvary* to mean any experience involving intense pain, anguish, and suffering (Matt. 27:33 and Lk. 23:33). Christ's suffering and death on Calvary was living proof that He gave His life and heart to us and for us because all were lost (dead) in trespasses and sin. *"For the love of Christ constraineth us, because we judge that, if one died for all, then we were all dead; and that He died for all, that they who live should not henceforth live unto themselves, but unto Him who died for them and rose again"* (Rom. 5:6-8, 14:8-9 and Eph. 2:1-10).

The Heart of the Cross of Jesus Christ was/is our exit door from God's wrath, sin, death, hell, eternal judgment, and condemnation. If we listen intently to *The Heart of the Cross*, we can still hear these heart cries of Jesus Christ to God His Father as He faced the death of the cross as the Lamb of God.

1. *Father! If you are willing, remove this cup from me; nevertheless not my will, but thine* (your will) *be done.* (Lk. 22:42)
2. *Father! That they may be one in us as we are one, that they may be made perfect in one.* (Jn. 17:18-23)
3. *Father! Forgive them; For they know not what they do.* (Lk. 23:43)
4. *My God, My God! Why have You forsaken Me?* (Mk. 15:34)
5. *Father! Into thy hands I commend my Spirit.* (Lk. 23:46)

Christ is our sacred heart (the Lord of Hearts) who was firmly fastened (attached, secured, nailed, pinned) to His cross, just as our natural heart within us is fixed firmly in position. In Philippians 2:6-8, we read that Jesus Christ was in the form of God and took upon Himself the form of a servant and was made (begotten) in the likeness of men. He was pierced in His Heart (Jn. 19:34-37, Rev. 1:7) and cut as in circumcision of the heart (Rom. 2:25-30). He humbled Himself and became obedient unto death, the horrible death of the cross! He was bruised, beaten, and wounded (Zech. 13:6-7) and yet many onlookers failed to discern that on the cross in the middle was no less than *God the Son in the midst of them.*

The mountains did tremble and the earth did quake (shake,

move). As they crucified the Son of God, no doubt the Heart of God the Father was driven to its maximum levels of love, mercy, grace, brokenness, forgiveness, and restraint, being held together only by His great love for sinful man. It has been said among many leaders that Christ was crucified and died upon a tree He Himself had designed and created in creation. The people mocked (ridiculed, made fun of, challenged, derided) Him. They had beaten Him beyond recognition, pulled out His hair by the roots, drove a crown of thorns into His skull, spat on Him and drove great nails into His hands and feet. Yet He remained (and remains today) our only living sacrifice, Redeemer, Savior, and sin offering acceptable to God (Eph. 5:1-2). For the first and last time, the will and Heart of God stood in its finished position just as Christ had spoken in John 17:4 and 19:30. The people who voted to kill Him looked upon the cross, believing the nails driven into His hands and feet held Him fast, but in truth it was His great love, His tender, merciful, and grace-filled heart for sinful man. As the Roman soldiers drove the great nails through His hands and feet, forgiveness for all sin was established and all enmity (hatred, malice, ill will, animosity) and separation between God and man were cancelled. Those ordinances and trespasses that stood against us were abolished. They were all blotted out and nailed to the Cross of Christ (Eph. 2:14-16 and Col. 2:13-15), and the devil was forever defeated. In Isaiah 52:14, the Prophet Isaiah saw *The Heart of the Cross* and wrote this, saying: "*Many were astounded because his visage was so marred* (bruised, defaced, injured, damaged, disfigured) *more than any man, and his form* (body) *more than the sons of men.*" We can take this to mean that He was hardly recognizable as a human being (See Is. 50:6 and 53:1-12).

There was also much breaking upon Calvary such as the breaking of all sin, sickness, and disease. The breaking of the evil and dark powers of death, hell, and the grave. The breaking of Satan's power, purpose, plans, and ordinances that held us captive and laws that separated us from a right relationship with God were also blotted out. Most assuredly with all of His heart He gave His love, heart, and life for us that we may be able to give our lives and love to Him as required. He loved us unto the end. (Jn. 13:1-4, 18:37, and Rom. 14:7-9)

In Isaiah 53:6-12, the Prophet Isaiah continued to write about his vision of *The Heart of the Cross*, giving mankind a clear view (picture, purpose) of the greatest future event in history yet to come.

- Verse 6: He carried our peace, and by His stripes we are/were healed.
- Verse 7: He was oppressed and afflicted.
- Verse 8: He was cut off from the land of the living and stricken for our transgressions.
- Verse 10: His soul was made an offering for sin.
- Verse 11: He bore our iniquities for our justification.
- Verse 12: He poured out His soul unto death. He bore the sins of many and made intercession for our transgressions.

"And it was about the sixth hour and there was a darkness over all the earth until the ninth hour. And the sun was darkened (refused to shine) *and the veil of the temple was rent* (torn) *in the midst from top to bottom. And when Jesus had cried with a loud voice, He said; 'Father, into thy hands I commend my spirit.' Having said this, He gave up the spirit."* (Lk. 23:-44-46) It is now written upon the pages of time that Jesus Christ is the only man ever crucified who stopped His own lungs from breathing and His heart from beating. He hung His head and died by His own power. For the first and only time, He became breathless. His body became lifeless, even though He was/is the *Breath of Life* (Gen. 2:7 and 7:15 and 22).

All things that live and move upon the face of the earth and breathe have hearts and inner breathing systems, yet at the point of death the Lord became breathless. He drew death unto Himself so it would be defeated also. Christ's resurrection would be a returning to breath, He would breathe again. While our lungs are important respiratory organs in the thorax of vertebrates that oxygenate the blood and remove carbon dioxide from it, the heart is the true breath-a-lizer; our air, blood and water pump and distribution center of both our natural (finite) and spiritual (infinite) life. There is a great difference between natural and spiritual breath. Breathing is what we do, breath is the substance and power of it. It isn't just what we breathe in that matters most, but also those things that we breathe forth out of our spirits and hearts, such as hate, cursing, blasphemy, and wrong, sinful words that are defiled and unclean. Let us not forget that the wages of sin is death (breathlessness). Christ had to die for us so that by the *Heart of the Cross* we could breathe clean, eternal breath in Him, the breath of life.

Job 33:4 says this: "*The Spirit of God hath made me, and the breath of the Almighty hath given me life."* While we give thanks unto God for many wonderful blessings, let us give thanks unto Him for breath and pray that more breath ministries will be established today in the land. The Apostle Paul spoke of breath, wherein we breathe, inhale, draw in air and exhale (breathe out). *"God, who made the world and all things in it, seeing that He is Lord of Heaven and earth, dwelleth not in temples made with hands, neither is worshipped with men's hands, as though He needed anything, seeing He giveth to all, life and breath, and all things. For in Him we live, move and have our being."* (Study Acts 17:22-31)

In Adam all died, but in Christ and by His resurrection to breath, all were made alive (1 Cor. 15:22). Born as lost sinners, we were spiritually breathless until we came to the *Heart of the Cross* of Jesus Christ and received new breath by His resurrection to life on the third day (Matt. 8:21-22). We are now free from death and breathlessness. In John 20:21-22, Jesus came to His disciples, He <u>breathed on them</u> and said unto them: *"Receive ye the Holy Ghost (Spirit)."* Though every one of them were breathing common air, they needed spiritual breath that would come unto them by the cross, a breath of God, as the breath (wind) on the day of Pentecost (Acts 2:1-5). Far too many churches and denominations are as breathless, void of spiritual breath. Satan has deceitfully taken their breath away and the *Heart of the Cross* is not there. Without a spiritual breath impartation and breath empowerment unto life through and by the cross, many are already dead, caused by man's religion, doctrines, traditions, distant hearts, blind and breathless money mongrels, con artists, beggars being led by the spirit of mammon. Yet let everything that has breath praise ye the Lord (Ps. 150:5).

Let us profile some things that were birthed, established, and abolished by the living sacrifice of our Lord and Savior Jesus Christ that flowed from *The Heart of the Cross*.

- The power of Satan, death, hell, and the grave was defeated (1 Cor. 15:55 and 2 Tim. 1:10) (See also Matt. 27:52-53)
- A new heart covenant was established (Eze. 11:19-21 and 36:26)
- A new blood covenant and testimony came unto being (2 Tim. 1:8-10 and Rev. 1:1-9)
- All sickness and disease were healed (Is. 53:5 and 1 Pet. 2:24)
- Our weakness was made strong (2 Cor. 13:4)
- The fulfillment of the law was completed (Col. 2:14 and Matt. 5:17-

18) Note: The law was changed from tablets of stone to the tablets of man's heart by a new covenant (Heb. 10:16-17), a new and living way
- Fear of death, hell and the grave was removed (2 Tim. 1:2-10 and Heb. 2:14-18), death was abolished, and salvation, life and immortality were established
- All hatred and animosity were erased (Jn. 15:18-25 and Jn. 3:13-14)
- Power (authority) was given to believers for them to overcome all evil temptation and lusts (Heb. 2:18 and 4:15)
- A New Testament and a new covenant were birthed (Mk. 14:24-25 and 1 Cor. 11:25)
- All sin, wrong and unrighteousness were forgiven (Deut. 25:16, 2 Thess. 2:10-12 and 1 Jn. 1:9)
- Our victory over Satan and all evil was established (Jn. 19:30 and Col. 2:15)
- All curses were removed (Deut. 21:22-23 and Gal. 3:13-14)
- The Kingdom of Heaven had come down to Earth (Matt. 4:17) and the Kingdom of God within man's heart
- Our sin debt and iniquities were paid (Rom. 4:7)
- Our guilt, blame and shame were removed (Heb. 12:2)
- Man's salvation by grace through faith was confirmed (Lk. 2:30 and 3:6)
- The power of salvation (Jn. 10:9-11, deliverance (Lk. 4:18, Acts 7:34) and healing (Ps. 107:20 and Matt. 9:35) was given to the church
- The abundance of new life in Christ was established (Jn. 10:10)
- Satan and his power, plans, purpose, and kingdom were defeated (Lk. 4:3-13, Jn. 8:51, 11:25-26 and Rom. 6:16-23)
- Eternal life was given to all who would believe and receive Him (Jn. 6:54, 17:2-3, Rom. 6:23 and 1 Jn. 5:11-20)
- The church (body of Christ) was established (Matt: 16:13-19 and 1 Cor. 12:18-27)
- The nine gifts of the Spirit (1 Cor. 12:7-10), the nine fruit of the Spirit (Gal. 5:22-23) and the five-fold gifts of apostles, prophets, evangelists, pastors, and teachers were given and established as free gifts (Eph. 4:11-12)

All of these came forth by the cross and were spiritually heart-designed, received, and heart-operated through love. Who would not serve a God like this?

In 1 Corinthians 1:17-18, the Apostle Paul stated that the preaching of the cross is the power of God. Again in 1 Corinthians 2:2, he states he chose to know nothing except Jesus Christ and Him crucified. Apparently, Paul knew Jesus Christ was our only substitute wherein He took our place on Calvary; He became our replacement (supplanter). All mankind was guilty of sin, worthy of death, and deserving of hell and the grave, but because of the substitutionary work on Calvary in taking our place, we have been set free and enjoy a free salvation, a free life, and a *free heart*.

But God commendeth His love towards us in that while we were yet sinners, Christ died for us (Rom. 5:8). Through substitution, Christ also fulfilled the law of restitution that states when a debt (or sin) has been paid for the guilty, they are set free, never to return, and they can never be judged or sentenced for the same debt or crime (Rom. 6:10). *"For He hath made Him, who knew no sin, to be sin for us that we might be made the righteousness of God in Him"* (2 Cor. 5:21) By God's Agape love, kindness, pity, and compassion, His true heart on Calvary was shown unto all mankind in its fullness. Jesus Christ became our advocate (vindicator, defender, supporter) (1 Jn. 2:1), the propitiation (atonement, conciliation, appeasement) required for our sins, our sin debt and payment. (1 Jn. 2:2 and 4:10). He has saved us to the utmost. No one or nothing can pluck (pick, draw, jerk, grab, uproot) us out of His hands (Jn. 10:22-30). God's grace will never take us where His mercy cannot find us and restore us. We are chained by His grace and shackled by His mercy. By *The Heart of the Cross* we have a better covenant and testament above the Law and the Ten Commandments of Moses (Heb. 7:19-22, 8:6, and 9:23). Why is this? The Old Testament was from the outside in, but from *The Heart of the Cross* it flows from the inside out. We are covered and purchased by the blood of the Lamb of God, our names written in the Lamb's Book of Life. We are born again, our hearts are God's dwelling place, God's heart is our dwelling place, and we have crossed over from finite humanity to infinite godliness as God's bride, His earthly body and Kingdom. By His great grace we are heirs and joint-heirs with Christ, walking in victory, daily washed by God through faith (Acts 15:8-9) by the Word of God (Jn. 15:3) and the blood of the Lamb (Rev. 1:5). We are enjoying a changed heart, a new heart, a right and renewed mind. We walk by faith in Christ and He in us (Jn. 14:20, 15:3-7 and 17:21-23). We have new breath and new life. This is the honor, life and glory of *The Heart of the Cross*. Here are some *Heart types of the Cross of Jesus Christ* that are free for the asking, that we may fulfill our earthly calling, purpose, and assignment. These come perfected and complete, having God's approval by the death, burial, and resurrection of Jesus Christ. All are firmly cross-connected and do manifest themselves as we *take up our cross and follow Him*.

Top of cross:
- Obedient: Romans 6:1 and Philippians 2:8
- Faithful: Nehemiah 9:8 and 1st Corinthians 10:13
- Forgiving: Acts 8:22, Colossians 3:12, 1st John 1:9 and 2:12
- Humble: Philippians 2:8
- Willing: Exodus 35:5-22, 1st Chronicles 28:9 and 29:9

Left arm of cross:
- Meek & Lowly: Matthew 11:29 and 1st Peter 3:4
- True: Jeremiah 10:10 and Hebrews 10:22
- Understanding: 1st Kings 3:9-12, Proverbs 2:2, 8:5, Job 38:26 and Ecclesiastes 1:6
- Tender: 2 Kings 22:19 and Ephesians 4:32
- Sound: Psalm 119:80, Proverbs 14:30 and Jeremiah 48:36

Center of cross:
- Loving: Mark 12:28-33, John 13:1 and 34-35
- Clean: John 15:3, Psalm 51:10 and 73:1
- Trusting: Psalm 28:7 and Proverbs 31:11

Right arm of cross:
- Perfect: 1st Kings 8:61 and Matthew 5:48
- Word Filled: Psalm 119:1 and Jeremiah 20:9
- Honest: Luke 8:15 and 1 Timothy 2:2
- Right: 2 Kings 10:15 and Ezekiel 13:22
- Wisdom Filled: 2 Chronicles 9:23 and Proverbs 14:33

Bottom of cross:
- Praying: 2 Samuel 7:27, John 17:1-6 and James 5:13-16
- Blameless: Ephesians 1:4-7 and 2 Peter 3:14
- Circumcised: Deuteronomy 10:16 and Romans 2:18-29
- Good: Luke 6:43-45
- Pure: Matthew 5:8, 1 Timothy 1:5 and 2 Timothy 2:22

Chapter 3
The Blood And Water Of The Cross

"*But when they came to Jesus and saw that He was dead already, they broke not His legs; but one of the soldiers with a spear pierced His side* (heart) *and immediately came there out blood and water*" (Jn. 19:33-34). Most Christians have been taught of the blood of the Cross of Christ, but few have learned of the water that also came forth as a river of life. As the Roman soldier thrust his great spear through the heart of Jesus Christ, the people saw blood and water that came forth out of His body.

Not only did natural water and blood come forth that could be seen, but also <u>spiritual blood and water</u> that could not be seen by the naked eyes of those standing there. Revelation reveals that unto God blood has a voice. It does speak. When Cain, the son of Adam and Eve, killed his brother, Abel, God spoke to Cain, saying: "*What have thou done? The voice of thy brother's blood crieth unto me from the ground*" (Gen. 4:10). The waters do roar their voice (Ps. 46:3) and blood cries out expressly, yet none standing by at the Cross of Christ could hear what the blood and water were saying as they flowed forth from the cross from the body of Christ as He hung there in nakedness and shame on Calvary. From the cross blood and water went out unto all the Earth and was made available unto all who would believe, be saved, and become a member of the Body of Christ. In the beginning, before the creation of man, the Holy Spirit "*moved upon the face of the waters*" (Gen. 1:1-8).

<u>Natural water</u> is seen as H_2O, a colorless, transparent liquid as rivers, oceans, and lakes, and hydrogen and oxygen that falls from the clouds as rain. It may be ice, steam, fog, snow, tears, urine, saliva, and the fluid that surrounds the fetus during pregnancy. In <u>water baptism,</u> Jesus was baptized in natural water by John the Baptist, even though He Himself was water as a fountain of life who came to this earth by blood and water. Just as natural man cannot live without blood and water, neither can our spiritual man live without the spiritual blood of Calvary and God's holy water of life, Jesus Christ being our fountain (Ps. 36:9, Jer. 2:13) and our source (Jn. 4:14,

1Jn. 5:6-8).

In Acts 2:38, the Apostle Peter instructed all to repent and be baptized in water in the name of Jesus Christ for the remission of sins. Jesus spoke to Nicodemus in John 3:5, saying, "*Verily, verily, I say unto you, except a man be born of Water and of the Spirit he cannot enter into the Kingdom of God.*" In John 4:5-15, He spoke to the woman at the well of the infinite spiritual water that is far greater than the finite water that was in the well. This was/is the same water that would flow profusely out of Him on Calvary, into and out of all those who would believe (Jn. 7:39-41).

In the birthing process of both natural and spiritual children, there is water, spirit (breath), and blood. Therefore, we must believe through faith in the blood and water of Jesus Christ that we have our new spiritual birth (Jn. 3:3-5), our new born again creature (2 Cor. 5:17), a new heart and spirit (Eze. 11:19 and 18:31), even a new man and person (Eph. 2:15 and 4:24). (See also Acts 17:22-29) The blood of Jesus is simply awesome in the workings of our new covenant, heart, and life in Christ. Hebrews 9:11-26 speaks of His shed blood and how it gives us eternal redemption. It purges (exterminates, removes, purifies) our conscience from dead works, it solidifies our New Testament and Commandments, and we have the remission (relief, breaking, pardon, forgiveness, mercy and acquittal) of all sins. (See Matt. 26:27-28) What a great hope this is for the pure in heart (Matt. 5:8 and 1 Jn. 3:3). We have been made sin-free within our spirit (Rom. 6:18-22).

While we are on this page, let us go to the beginning of creation and take a closer look at the blood. In Genesis 2:21-25, God put Adam to sleep, took one of his ribs, and made a woman, because she was taken out of man. Today we know the bones are the place where our blood is made. Adam called Eve "bone of his bones, and flesh of his flesh," not knowing that she was also "blood of his blood." Adam was formed from the ground, Eve was from the blood of his bones, so all who would be born upon the earth would be birthed by the blood seed of an earthly man, except Jesus Christ. Satan the sinner came forth, and with deceitful, lying words deceived Eve, wherein sin did enter into the bloodlines of both Adam and Eve, for they were one blood. Though Adam and Eve sewed fig leaves together to cover themselves, it was not enough. Their DNA (genetic code, family tree, seed, heredity information, genes, templates) was now filled with sin and death, their blood was thoroughly contaminated (defiled, polluted, corrupt, infected), and all their offspring would be born in sin and unto death. Mankind was disconnected (separated) from God's plan, purpose, and provision. Spiritually speaking, they both died that day as God said they would. God came down into the garden, killed a lamb, and covered them with its wool and blood as an atonement for their souls until the cross of His Son Jesus Christ. In Genesis 5:1-2, God reveals the name of both Adam and Eve was <u>Adam</u>. When Adam blamed Eve for this travesty, he was actually blaming himself. This was because they were both of one blood. Their life was in the blood (Lev. 17:10-16 and 1 Cor. 15:50). Yet God had another Adam in His bosom and He was called the *Last Adam*.

The last Adam came forth into Mary's womb, characterized (formed) by the Holy Spirit with pure water and the perfect blood of God (Lk. 1:26-38 and 1 Jn. 5:6), not the imperfect blood and water of Mary. Because life is in the blood and water, the *Last Adam* on Calvary would give His blood and water unto the whole world that we might be blood-purchased, redeemed, and water-washed. We see the *Last Adam* written by the Apostle Paul in 1 Corinthians 15:45: *"And so it is written, the first man, Adam, was made a living soul from the ground, the last Adam was made a life-giving* (quickening) *spirit."* Also in 1 Corinthians 15:47: *"the first man is of the earth, earthly; the second man is the Lord from Heaven."* (See also Gen. 2:7)

In Acts 17:28-29, the Apostle Paul writes, saying: *"For in Him we live and move, and have our being; For we are also His offspring. Forasmuch, then, as we are the offspring of God; we ought not to think that the Godhead is like gold or silver or stone, carved by art and man's device."* Through the blood and the *Heart of the Cross*, we have been redeemed and reconnected to God, having a new Book of Life (Phil. 4:3, Rev. 20:12-15), Word of Life (1 Jn. 1:1), and <u>Water of Life</u> (Rev. 21:6), wherein we are deeply anchored, firmly molded, divinely rooted and saved by the cross of the Last Adam.

On Calvary new life flowed from the cross, grace (favor) restored man's fellowship with God, and a new heart became available for a new relationship. Being born of the blood and water of the cross, we have been brought back into <u>fellowship</u> with God (1 Cor. 1:9 and 1 Jn. 1:3-7). Jesus Christ (God the Word) came forth from God the Father that through death He may give us new life by His Spirit (Rom. 8:8-10). His precious blood and living waters are as many rivers flowing out of our hearts. This is He who came by water and blood, even Jesus Christ, not by water only, but by <u>water and blood.

"*For there are three that bear record in Heaven; the Father, the Word, and the Holy Spirit and these three are one. There are three that bear witness in earth; the Spirit, and the Water, and the Blood and these three agree in one*" (1 Jn. 5:5-8). Revelation reveals through understanding here that the Father, the Word, the Holy Spirit, the water, and the blood were all there at the crucifixion of Jesus Christ as a witness for the Word and Will of God. Let us view some concepts and meanings of the blood.

Blood is a vital fluid found in our circulatory system. It is naturally known as lifeblood, heart's blood, vital juices, life fluid, plasma, and serum. It is also connected to our lineage, DNA heritage, ancestry, birth, and family line. It may be seen as the bad blood of a culprit, hatred, malice, feud, anger, and rancor; also as being cold, deliberate, willfull, heartless, cruel, ruthless, and brutal. Some people are viewed as being bloodless, which is also coldhearted, unemotional, unfeeling, unkind, indifferent, listless, lazy, and slow. On Calvary's hill there was bloodshed, indicating slaughter, butchery, killing, blood bath, carnage, massacre, and murder. Some evil persons are listed as being bloodthirsty, having a murderous heart and a ruthless mind, being homicidal, savage, ruthless, cruel, fierce, inhuman, and murderous. In the natural realm, the people saw Christ and His cross were bloody, bleeding, bloodstained, gory, grisly, crimson, wounded, gaping, open, dripping blood, raw, blood-soaked, and as of hemorrhaging. The Father testifies of creation, the Word testifies of all the works of God, and the Holy Spirit of His grace, love, mighty power, and breath. The water from the cross testifies of a new life, and the blood a new birthing and cleansing, purchasing His bride the Church. "*Take heed, therefore, unto yourselves, and to all the flock, over which the Holy Spirit hath made you overseers, to feed the Church of God which He hath purchased with His own blood*" (Acts 20:28). (See also Heb. 9:24-28) The Lord's spiritual blood washes and cleanses us (1 Jn. 1:7) as well as the Word (Jn. 15:3). We were all an unclean (defiled) thing, but are washed by the blood of Jesus Christ; the water also washes us (Acts 22:16, Eph. 5:26 and Heb. 10:22). Spirit, blood and water determine our natural and spiritual life in Jesus Christ.

If there is to be a true manifestation of salvation, miracles, deliverance, healing and birthing of ministries, the presence of God's Spirit, water, word, and blood is mandatory. It is important that we keep a Christ-filled (word-filled), water-filled, blood-filled, and spiritually filled heart. In John 6:53-56, Jesus said: *"Except ye eat the flesh of the Son of Man, and drink His blood, ye have no life in you. He who eateth my flesh, and drinketh my blood, hath eternal life; and I will raise him up the last day. For my flesh is food indeed and my blood is drink indeed. He that eateth my flesh* (the bread of life) *and drinketh my blood* (the source of life) *dwelleth in me, and I in him."* We are made nigh (drawn close to God) by the blood of the cross (Eph. 2:13) that was given for the washing and cleansing so that all may stand before Him pure and clean having a *blood-washed heart.* Who is that person who stands in God's presence to worship, sing, and give thanks, having an unclean heart, a dirty mind, a contaminated and polluted soul? The good news is the fact that the blood of the cross can make the most vile sinner clean. To our hurt and shame, most of us do not see ourselves as being blood-bought, blood-washed, and blood-covered in Christ by the cross. We have seen in John 7:38-39 how Christ declared that out of our heart (essence, center, core, root), which may also be out of our spirit (substance, intellect, motivation), our being (existence, presence, life, creature, individual), shall flow rivers of living water; life water, His Spirit as water.

As we open our mouths wide unto God, He fills our hearts with living water, His Spirit, blood, and Word (Ps. 81:10-12). Why does God look on and fill our hearts? The heart cannot perform its duties without the presence and flowing of blood. Blood and water can only stand still for a short time, both must be continually kept flowing, or they will soon spoil, evaporate, or decay. There has to be a power or force to propel them forth in both our natural and spiritual bodies and lives. That power, place, and force is the heart. This is another reason why God looks on the heart. His spiritual electrocardiogram (EKG) is at work without ceasing as our Great Physician. He must make sure the right amount of blood, word, spirit, air, and water is flowing in and out of it. In natural flesh man, blood and water make up over 70 percent of our body. In natural living, having a washday is a very important day. When we wash our clothes in water, we use detergents, and for the most unclean we add bleach. We expect and demand our prize possessions to be clean. In the washing of our automobiles, food, bodies, and homes, we are faithful and diligent, always seeking perfect cleanliness. How much more important is it for us to stand spiritually clean, pure, and holy in our hearts and minds before our God! In Jeremiah 4:14, God cried out through His prophet Jeremiah unto all Israel, saying: O Jerusalem, wash thine heart from wickedness, that thou mayest be saved. In Matthew 23:25-28, Jesus scolded the religious leaders, telling them how they diligently cleanse the outside of a cup (their body) but fail to cleanse the inside that's filthy, dirty, unclean, and full of hypocrisy and iniquity. Even in our daily walk of life, inner cleansing is a most important thing that we may live free from sickness and disease, which are all unclean. By the washing of water, blood, and the Word of God, we are spiritually cleansed, filled, approved of God and kept alive as sin-free in Christ. It is a matter of faith. Spiritually we need the blood and water of the cross. God also uses our faith as a cleanser to keep us clean.

He puts no difference between us, both Jew and Gentile, purifying our hearts by faith (Acts 15:9), and giving to us the remission of sins by the shed blood of Jesus Christ (Matt. 26:26-28). In every hospital on earth, physicians require a blood test before treatments can take place. They must know our blood pressure levels, and in serious situations our blood type. We may consider the blood to be the oil within our inner engine of life, called the heart. What great things that He (God) has done and is doing for us. *"Jesus Christ who is the faithful witness, and the first begotten of the dead, and the Prince of the King of the earth. Unto Him that loved us and washed us from our sins in His own blood"* (Rev. 1:5). (See also Rev. 5:8-10 and 7:14) By the washing of blood and by the washing of the Word as water, our guilt and shame have been and are removed (Heb. 12:1-2). As cross bearers we have been pronounced Not Guilty.

"But if we walk in the light, as he is in the light, we have fellowship one with another, and the blood of Jesus Christ, His Son, cleanses us from all sin" (1 Jn. 1:7). (See also Rev. 7:14) Because all have sinned (Rom. 3:23), all must be blood-purchased, washed, and cleansed, because of the uncleanliness of sin and our vile, polluted, and defiled flesh. Cleanliness is next to godliness and holiness, and without holiness can no man see the Lord (Heb. 12:14). David cried out unto God for a clean heart in Psalm 51:10. By the blood of the cross, we are made cleaner than clean and purer than pure. As Republicans and Democrats wrestle with America's national debt, few realize that the greatest debt in all the earth was/is our sin debt, which was paid in full by Jesus Christ on Calvary. Because of the rejection of the *Heart of the Cross*, sin is America's greatest problem. The shedding of blood and water on Calvary was the true debt cancellation from God. His

blood is sinless, our overcoming power, victory, and great spiritual weapon. It prevails over all demonic powers and Satan. While we have several blood types on earth, God's blood type is not fully known. We know it is holy, rare, flows from Calvary, is eternal, will never lose its power, and is the power of our salvation. Blood flow is crucial to life. Loss of blood flow means loss of air, water, vital nutrients, life, and soon the stoppage of our hearts. Praise be to God, the blood still works!

Because of sin, unclean hearts, carnality, and immorality, we cannot stand in Jehovah's presence, swim in His living waters, or be filled with holy rivers of living waters. Without the cleansing word, cleansing faith, and washing of blood and water that flows from *The Heart of the Cross*, God's salvation alone cannot save us. It is predicated upon the blood of the cross. Without God's cleansing blood and a beating, pure heart, we have no life and breath in Christ. Where there is blood, there is grace, breath, power, living life water, which is the blood, air, and water system; the lungs as a channel (conduit), the heart as a reservoir (storage). Through Christ's blood, His word, and water flowing, and by the lifting of Jesus Christ on Calvary, the Lord draws all men unto Himself. "*And I, if I be lifted up from the earth, I will draw all men* (and judgment) *unto me*" (Jn. 12:32). (See also Eph. 2:13) He draws us unto Himself, as a shepherd does his sheep, our spiritual heart that was dead (lost) now comes alive. It begins to function as a blood, water, and air pump for a great flowing and gushing forth of blood, living water, and the breath of God. We are changed, transformed, born again by the written word in our heart and the Living Word, who is also a spiritual fountain of water, our blood donor, the breath of life; namely the Lord Jesus Christ.

In Revelation 19:13, the Apostle John being caught up unto Heaven, saw Him, and wrote: "*And He was clothed with a vesture dipped in blood; and His name is called THE WORD OF GOD!*" (See also Rev. 12:11)

Second only to our heart covenant found in Ezekiel 11:19-21 and 36:26, is the blood covenant found in Hebrews 10:16-29 and 13:20-21, wherein we are washed, made free, and kept sin-free in God's presence. Let us not forget that in the Old Testament (Ex. 12:12-30), Pharaoh would not let Israel go out from Egypt. God commanded Moses and Israel to put lamb's blood upon the doors of their houses for the judgment of Pharaoh and for Israel's redemption, atonement, and Passover. God's confession of the blood of the slain lambs was this: *"and when I see the blood I will <u>Pass Over You</u>. I will not allow the destroyer to destroy you and your families."* Israel, like unto us, was saved by the blood of a slain lamb. But the firstborn of Egypt and Pharaoh died that very night. All Israel now had direct access to God by what is known as "The Passover." Let us view some great benefits freely given to us today by the blood and water that came forth from *The Heart of the Cross*, from the very heart of Jesus Christ.

- **We were redeemed (Redemption):** Which means to recover through payment. A ransom paid. To be rescued through recovery. To buy back. Repurchase. Repay. Regain and reclaim. To be rescued by the death, burial, and resurrection of Jesus Christ and set free. He redeemed us from all curses. *"Christ has redeemed us from the curse of the law, being made a curse for us; for it is written, cursed is everyone that hangeth on a tree"* (Gal. 3:13). (See also Ps. 103:1-5, Eph. 1:3-14, Tit. 2:13-14, and Col. 1:13-14) Forasmuch as you know you were not redeemed with corruptible things like silver and gold, but with the precious blood of Christ, as of a lamb without blemish and without spot (1 Pet. 1:18-19). (See also Ps. 107:2, 111:9, and Rev. 5:9) Jesus Christ is our redeemer (Job 19:25 and Jer. 50:34). Our blood donor (Rev. 19:13). By this all believers have a great redemption. *"In whom we have redemption through His blood, the forgiveness of sins according to the riches of His grace"* (Eph. 1:7, Col. 1:14, and Heb. 9:11-12). This is a great revelation. God's redeeming blood and water still flow from the heart of God unto all who believe.
- **We were reconciled (Reconciliation):** Reunited, reassigned, readjusted and brought together again with God. Propitiated (Rom. 3:25, 1 Jn. 2:2, and 4:10); settled, adapted, and appeased. *"While we were yet sinners Christ died for us. Much more then, being now justified by His blood, we shall be saved from wrath through Him. For as when we were enemies, we were <u>reconciled to God</u> by the death of His Son, much more, being reconciled, we shall be saved by His life"* (Rom. 5:10-11). (See also Col. 1:20-22) Our being drawn by the Holy Spirit to God is a great blessing, a great work and revelation of divine reconciliation. *"Therefore, if any man be in Christ, he is a new creature. Old things are passed away, behold all things are become new. And all things are of God, who hath <u>reconciled us to Himself</u> by Jesus Christ and hath given to us the ministry of reconciliation. God was in Christ reconciling the world unto Himself, not imputing their trespasses unto them and hath committed unto us the word of*

reconciliation" (2 Cor. 5:17-19). By our cross bearing and the Cross of Jesus Christ we have received the saving power and the grace of God in a finished position.

- **We were justified (Justification):** This means to be excused from guilt and sin, exonerated, defended, acquitted, vindicated, approved and cleared. By the process of justification through the blood and water of the cross, sinful man is made acceptable to a holy God. We are seen by God as guiltless. *"Therefore, being justified by faith, we have peace with God through our Lord Jesus Christ. Much more then, being now justified by His blood, we shall be saved from wrath through Him"* (Rom. 5:1 and 9). (See also Is. 53:11, Rom. 4:1-8, 25, and Tit. 3:7) *"Moreover, who He did predestinate, them He also called; and whom He called, them He also justified; and who He justified, them He also glorified"* (Rom. 8:30). (See also 1 Cor. 6:9-11, Gal. 3:8 and 24) Through justification, we become holiness of God in Christ (2 Cor. 5:21), and also through righteousness, we become holiness unto God (1 Pet. 1:16, Rom. 6:19-22 and 1 Thess. 3:13). Our justification is mandatory, for without it there can be no righteousness or holiness and no one unjustified shall see the Lord (Heb. 12:14).

- **We were sanctified (Sanctification:** This mean to be purified, cleansed and set apart from sin for the service of God on a daily continual basis. Through sanctification we are made pure, anointed, blessed, and fully dedicated to God. By the flowing blood and water of the cross of Christ, we are able to stand pure, consecrated, dedicated, and approved of God. This is because from Calvary He has forgiven us and washed us from our sins in His own blood (Rev. 1:5 and 1 Jn. 1:7). In speaking to the Apostle Paul concerning his purpose and ministry to both Jews and Gentiles, Yeshua the Lord said this: *"I have chosen thee to open their eyes, and to turn them from darkness to light, and from the power of Satan unto God, that they may receive forgiveness of sins and inheritance among them who are sanctified by faith that is in me"* (Acts 26:18). The Holy Spirit of God works to sanctify all who believe (Rom. 15:16). (See also Heb. 3:11 and 9:11-15). *"Know ye not that the unrighteous shall not inherit the Kingdom of God? Be not deceived, neither fornicators, nor idolaters, nor adulterers, nor effeminate, nor abusers of themselves with mankind, nor thieves, nor covetous, nor drunkards, nor revilers, nor extortionists, shall inherit in the Kingdom of God. And such were some of you; but you are washed, but you are* *sanctified, but you are justified in the name of the Lord Jesus, and by the Spirit of our God* " (1 Cor. 6:9-11). (See also 1 Cor. 1:2, 30-31, and 1 Pet. 3:15) Without the overflowing of righteousness, the watering of God's word, faith, and the cleansing streams of sanctification that give us clean minds, justification, and pure hearts, we may find ourselves enemies of the Cross of Christ. "*For many of whom I have told you often, and now tell you even weeping, that they are the enemies of the Cross of Christ*" (Phil. 3:17-18). It must be very clear that our perfection is firmly based upon the sacrifice and blood of Jesus Christ on Calvary (Heb. 10:14).

- **We were given the Propitiation:** This means to have freedom from sin and death by the atoning blood of Jesus Christ on the cross. Appeasement, conciliation, and pacification. By the works of these three, the shed blood of Jesus satisfied the penalty and paid the price for sin demanded by a holy God. The Bible teaches us that through propitiation, Christ took all our sins upon Himself and redeemed us from the penalty of death that the wages of our sins had demanded. (Lk. 18:13, Heb. 2:17) "*If any man sin, we have an advocate with the Father, Jesus Christ the righteous and He is the propitiation for our sins, and not for ours only, but also for the sins of the whole world*" (1 Jn. 2:1-2). "*Herein is love, not that we loved God, but that He loved us, and sent His Son to be the propitiation for our sins*" (1 Jn. 4:10 and Jn. 3:16). "*For all have sinned, and come short of the glory of God, being justified freely by His grace through the redemption that is in Christ Jesus. Whom God has sent forth to be a propitiation through faith in His blood, to declare His righteousness for the remission of sins that they are past, through the forbearance of God*" (Rom. 3:23-25). The word propitiation may also be interchangeable with the word atonement. Through propitiation (blood offering) and the suffering of Jesus Christ, we have the compensation, appeasement, and amendment of sins, victory, sin debt paid, and a new covenant of grace. God was satisfied. He took our sickness and gave us salvation, our diseases and gave us life. He bore our pains and gave us a new covenant relationship, wherein we are delivered from God's wrath to come. The power of sin to separate between God and man has been annulled. All mankind was sin-sick, sin-lost and dead in sin. By His stripes we are and were healed (Is. 53:5 and 1 Pet. 2:24). By all the above, it pleased the Lord to bruise His Son, put Him to grief on Calvary, and make His soul an offering for sin (Is. 52:14 and 53:10)

- **We have been restored (Restoration):** This means to make restitution, replace, put back, to reestablish, revive, recover, rebuild, reinstate, heal, and restore. Between Malachi and Matthew approximately 450 years transpired wherein God had nothing much to do with mankind. He had disconnected Himself, awaiting the birth of Jesus Christ, our Restorer and Restoration. In Psalm 23:3, David wrote: "*He restoreth my soul; He leadeth me in the paths of righteousness for His name's sake."* As Jesus walked among the people, He restored withered hands (Matt. 12:13), opened blind eyes (Mk. 8:25), and many were healed and returned to good health (Matt. 8:8-13, 16, and Lk. 8:43-56). Yet it would take more than physical restoration to reinstate man to God, it would take the Lord's resurrection from the grave for sinful man to be restored as God's inheritance, His sons and daughters. The Apostle Paul understood the works of Jesus on Calvary that did reconnect and restore man to God in the Spirit and revive him back to fellowship, relationship (sonship), and spiritual life. "*For as many as are led by the Spirit of God, they are the sons of God. For ye have not received the spirit of bondage again to fear; but ye have received the Spirit of adoption, whereby we cry, Abba Father. The Spirit Himself bears witness with our spirit, that we are the children of God; and if children, then heirs of God and joint heirs with Christ if so be that we suffer with Him, that we may also be glorified together"* (Rom. 8:14-17). (See also Matt. 19:29, Acts 20:32 and 26:18) We have "the atonement" which is inseparable from our harmony and unity with Him; to make amends, reparations, to have recompense and be shifted through the works of the cross. Atonement believers have been reinstated to a divine relationship and oneness with Yeshua El Shaddai, regardless of their sins and shortcomings. The atonement blood eliminates condemnation (Rom. 8:1) and our being enemies of and against God (Rom. 5:9-11). It assures us of reconciliation, restoration, a new covenant (Heb. 8:10 and 10:16-18), and a daily fresh flowing of Yeshua's cleansing blood as a river of life (Lev. 17:11 and 1:4). The atonement is a free gift of God, a sacrificial system wherein as believers we are now right with God through the death, burial, and resurrection of His Son. In the Old Testament, man received forgiveness by animal sacrifices of bulls, goats, and lambs, but under the new covenant we have all of these by His Son the sacrificial Lamb of God. (Heb. 9:12-15 and 10:4) *"And walk in love as Christ hath also loved us, and hath given Himself for us an offering and a sacrifice to God for a sweet smelling savor"* (Eph. 5:2 and 1 Pet. 1:19). Through atonement, we have forgiveness for the sins of our minds and hearts, which are many. For this we have the washing of regeneration (Tit. 3:5), inner revival (Rom. 14:9), a rebirthing (Jn. 3:3-5), reformation (Heb. 9:10), salvation and complete restoration. Truly the outflowing of blood and water from the heart of Jesus Christ on Calvary would draw all men unto Himself. With open arms, His voice may still be heard by every ear and heart, saying: *"Come, flow with me ye waters of my salvation and my blood will flow through you unto all the earth. You shall be mighty waters and rivers of life; living fountains, gushing forth that will never cease."*

- **We were forgiven (Forgiveness of sins):** An acquittal, pardon, mercy, and grace. We have been released, excused, and dismissed from eternal judgment. Through God's heart forgiveness, the articles of repentance, and the cross, we have received amnesty, remission of sins, clemency, and have been reinstated with God. *"Who have delivered us from the power of darkness and hath translated us into the Kingdom of His dear Son; in whom we have redemption through His blood, the forgiveness of sins"* (Col. 1:13-14, 2:13, 3:13, and 1 Jn. 2:12). As Jesus hung suspended between Heaven and hell upon the cross, He spoke to the Father. Then Jesus said: *"Father, forgive them; for they know not what they do. And they parted His raiment, and cast lots"* (Lk. 23:34). In writing to the Ephesian church, the Apostle Paul revealed and affirmed this: *"And be ye kind to one another, tenderhearted, forgiving one another, even as God, for Christ's sake has forgiven you"* (Eph. 4:32). (See also Ps. 103:1-4 and Eph. 1:3-7) Through forgiveness and a forgiving heart, we have direct access to God's heart, His Kingdom and eternal glory. It is also important that we pray, asking God to forgive us for our unforgiveness and the evil thoughts and wicked imagination of our own hearts (Acts 8:22).
- **We were saved (God's great salvation):** Salvation means to be rescued, removed from danger, set free, and protected. By the salvation works of the cross, wherein we are preserved, ransomed, reclaimed from death, hell, and the grave; regenerated, released, redeemed, and delivered from the power and penalty of sin (Rom. 3:23-25, 10:9, and Acts 4:12). *"For God so*

loved the world that He gave His only begotten Son, that whosoever believeth in Him should not perish, but have everlasting life. For God sent not His Son into the world to condemn the world, but that the world through Him might be saved" (Jn. 3:16-17). (See also Matt. 10:22, Lk. 8:12 and 2 Cor. 2:15) The Cross of Christ, and the fact that there is an empty tomb in Jerusalem assure us of God's great salvation. Christ has risen and has entered into the heart of man, which is His most holy place, His earthly address and kingdom. "*Wherefore, He is able to save them to the uttermost that come to God by Him, seeing He ever liveth to make intercession for them*" (Heb. 7:25). (See also Ps. 7:10-11, Eph. 2:5-8, and 1 Tim. 1:15) Revelation reveals that as we take up our cross daily, we become both debt- and death-free; being born again, having a new birth, a new covenant of blood, new life, breath, new heart, and a changed mind. Our salvation flows forth as a great river of life, unstoppable, overflowing unto all as waters of a most beautiful waterfall, as a deep sea, or gentle ocean that covers, having great waters that are powerful enough to quench all sin, the cold hands of death, the fires of hell, and the powers of the grave (Ps. 18:1-6, Is. 12:1-3, Matt. 10:22, Lk. 19:10, and Tit. 3:5). However, *biblical salvation* is required, not by any religion, denomination, man's theology, unbelief or doctrine. God is a winner and never a loser. He alone is the keeper of our souls and salvation, the only writer of our names in the Lamb's Book of Life. We have a personal relationship with God, His DNA, and our names are written in blood (in Christ) in the Lamb's Book of Life. For salvation (Christ) to say it is finished, there has to be repentance, exchanging our old heart for a new heart, being born again, and becoming a new creature in Christ, our soul anchored in the Lord, having a renewed mind and even a perfect heart, to contain His perfect love, Word, peace and God's perfect Son.

- **We became righteousness (unto God):** This mean to be in right standing, virtuous, moral, guiltless before God, devoted to a sinless life, upright, honest, goodhearted, godly, holy, and blameless (Ps. 15:2, Pr. 14:34, and Rom. 6:11-23). Through the death of Christ, we have been made the righteousness of God in Christ, fruitful trees of righteousness, standing and bearing much fruit unto God by the washing of living water of spiritual life (Is. 61:1-3). We are established in righteousness and watered through faith (Rom. 9:30, Phil. 3:9, and Heb. 11:7). Having full support of the waters of the cross with righteousness, we are now made right and not wrong, just and not unjust, godly not ungodly or unholy in heart. We are eternally blessed, having a pure, clean and washed heart, a right and renewed mind. As we hunger and thirst for the watering of God's presence and the bread of life, we must also hunger and thirst for righteousness. In Matthew 5:6, the Lord Jesus said this: "*Blessed are they who do hunger and thirst after righteousness; for they shall be filled.*" Again, He spoke giving us good instruction, saying: "*But seek ye first the Kingdom of God and His righteousness and all these things* (love, faith, salvation, eternal life, money, treasures, clothing, houses and land) *shall be added unto you*" (Matt. 6:33). While we look to be saved, to be in Heaven with Christ, let us not forget that we must first be made righteousness unto God through the blood and water of the Cross of Jesus Christ. "*For He* (God) *hath made Him* (Jesus), *who knew no sin, to be sin for us, that we be made the righteousness of God in Him*" (2 Cor. 5:21). (See also 1 Pet. 3:14 and 13:16) Righteousness exalts a nation, but sin is a reproach (blame, condemnation, wrong) to any people (Pr. 14:34). For God's approval, America must return to righteousness, seeking Him for a right heart. The issue and hindering spirits are sin, pride, and self-righteousness. We must look to the Cross of Christ daily with humility, honor, and respect to avoid the terrible state of self-righteousness that deceives us, and takes us out of God's will, purpose, blessings, and plans. The Apostle Paul in Philippians 3:7-9 stated that he counted all things as dung (refuse) that he might win Christ and "*be found in Him* (God's heart) *not having mine own righteousness, which is of the law, but that which is through the faith of Christ, the righteousness which is of God by faith.*" The Prophet Isaiah speaks of our iniquities and the uncleanness of all those who refuse to come to the cross's waters of life and be spiritually cleansed unto righteousness. "*But we are all as an unclean thing, and all our righteousness* (self-righteousness, too) *are as filthy rags; and we all do fade as a leaf, and our iniquities, like the wind, have taken us away*" (Is. 64:6). What then must we do to secure righteousness unto ourselves that assures us of eternal salvation? We open the doors of our hearts and open our mouths wide, allowing God to fill them with His grace, word, faith, right believing, Spirit, and love. In righteousness (a right mind) we flow with Christ and swim in the deep waters of His salvation and grace. *"That if thou shalt confess with thy mouth the Lord Jesus, and shall <u>believe in thine heart</u> that God hath raised Him from the dead, thou shalt be saved. For with the <u>heart man believeth unto righteousness</u> and with the mouth confession is made unto salvation"* (Rom. 10:9-10). (See also Ps. 15:1-3).

- **We became holiness (unto God):** This means to become <u>spiritually</u> perfect, sanctified, pure, untainted by evil or sin, sacred and consecrated unto God. While holiness has become a no-no word among many religions, it still rests upon those who hunger and thirst after righteousness, who drink daily of the blood and living waters flowing as a fountain from the Cross of Christ. Holiness helps us to be and become what is required for us to be in God's presence. It is not a religion, but a state of existence. Holy (holiness) is a law and also a commandment. In the law, God the Father spoke, saying: *"For I am the Lord your God; Therefore sanctify yourselves and ye shall be holy; for I am holy; For I am the Lord who bringeth you up out of the land of Egypt, to be your God; ye shall therefore be holy for I am holy"* (Lev. 11:44-45). In the new covenant, the Holy Spirit speaks: *"But as he who hath called you is holy, so <u>be ye holy</u> in all manner of life* (conversation), *because it is written, be ye holy; for I am holy"* (1 Pet. 1:15-16). The word <u>be</u> means to live, endure, abide, breathe, remain and occupy a position; and the word <u>holy</u> (holiness) further means to be good, just, godly, blessed, uncorrupt, spotless, and pure in heart. Therefore, wherever there is righteousness, we can be sure it came forth through the pathways, presence, works, and waterways of a pure heart of holiness. *"Having therefore these promises* (of eternal life, reconciliation, justification, and forgiveness), *dearly beloved let us cleanse ourselves from all filthiness of the flesh and spirit, <u>perfecting holiness</u> in the fear* (respect and honor) *of God"* (2 Cor. 7:1). (See also Lk. 1:74-75 and Heb. 12:10-15) We must seek the Lord for a holy heart, a pure, sound, and right mind. This is accomplished by the washing of blood and water from the cross and by the pure Word of God (Eph. 5:26-27). The writer of Hebrews saw the waters of holiness being polluted, in decline, and warned us saying: *"Follow peace with all means, and holiness, without which no man shall see the Lord"* (Heb. 12:14). (See also Is. 35:4-8). What then must be our expectation of God in holiness as we walk with the Lord as a virgin bride unto our eternal destiny? *"To the end He may <u>establish your hearts blameless</u>*

in holiness before God, even our Father, at the coming of our Lord Jesus Christ with all His saints" (1 Thess.3:13). (See also Jms. 5:8) We are commanded to worship the Lord in the beauty of holiness (1 Chron. 16:29 and Ps. 29:2). We are to serve Him in holiness and righteousness all the days of our lives (Lk. 1:74-75). We are to put on our new man that is created by God in righteousness and true holiness (Eph. 4:24 and Rom. 6:19-23). Holiness assures us that we are no longer defiled, no longer separated from God. A spiritual washing (Jer. 4:14) has taken place by our believing and trusting in the watering gospel of the Cross of Christ. There is no coagulation of doubt, blood clots of unbelief, or a desperate need for a new heart transplant or an emergency renewal. We are not in danger of heart failure (Gen. 42:48, Deut. 28:65, and Lk. 21:26). There is no shadow of turning (Deut. 29:18, and Jms. 1:17). Revelation reveals that God has not called us to uncleanness but unto holiness (1 Thess. 4:7). In true biblical holiness, we shall never turn back into this world system in our hearts (1 Sam. 17:32, Ps. 40:12, and Acts 7:39). Our spirit, heart, and mind shall not faint (i.e., fainting spells). (See Eze. 21:7 an Heb. 12:3).

In Matthew 5:48, Jesus cried out, saying: *"Be ye, therefore, perfect as your Father in Heaven is perfect."* God's word, love, blood, salvation, faith, peace, eternal life, heart and Heaven are all perfect, to name a few. Imperfection can never be in oneness with perfection. The perfect *Heart of the Cross* is given unto us. Being perfect in heart, we are kept clean by the blood (Rev. 1:5), faith (Acts 15:9), and the Word of God (Jn. 15:3). We are sanctified and have become the righteousness of God in Christ. Only God can make one perfect, for He alone is well able. The arms of the Lord are still open wide unto all, saying: *"Come, flow with me, drink of my waters and I will flow through you. I will be a mighty river of life unto you and to all your seed, a flowing stream and fountain of blood and water within you that shall never run dry."* We were once far away from the Lord but have been made near by the perfect blood of the cross (Eph. 2:13).

By the water of the cross, we meet God's mandatory purification requirements, which are purging by faith, filtering by the Word, disinfecting and washing by the blood of God where we are fully pardoned, perfected, made clean and forgiven. (See Acts 15:9, Tit. 2:14, Jms. 4:8, 1 Pet. 1:22, and 2 Jn. 3:3). We have a new birth, new lineage, genealogy, beginning (genesis), and a new start (Jn. 3:1-8,

Gal. 4:19-29, 1 Jn. 3:9, and 4:7). We have an eternal seal, security, confirmation, validation, authentication, certification, and the approval of God (Jn. 6:27, 2 Cor. 1:22, Eph. 1:13 and 4:30).

Chapter 4
The Resurrection Of Jesus Christ

Jesus, when He had cried again, with *"a loud voice, yielded up the spirit (breath). And, behold, the veil of the temple was torn in two from the top to the bottom; and the earth did quake, and the rocks did split; and the graves were opened; and many bodies of the saints that slept were raised, and came out of the graves after His resurrection, and went into the holy city, and appeared unto many. Now when the centurion, and they that were with him watching Jesus, saw the earth quake, and these things that were done they feared greatly, saying;* **Truly, this was the Son of God**" (Matt. 27:50-54).

Jesus Christ was lifted up unto death by the hands of evil men, but was taken from death by the loving hands and power of Almighty God. The Apostle Peter, on the day of Pentecost, stood up and spoke to Israel concerning Christ that He *"being delivered by the determinate counsel and foreknowledge of God, ye have taken, and by wicked hands have crucified and slain; whom God raised up, having loosed the pains of death, because it was not possible that He should be held by it"* (Acts 2:23-24). (See also Acts 4:10-12 and 5:29-32) I believe the real reason Satan, death, hell, and the grave could not hold back or stop the resurrection of Jesus Christ is found in Colossians 2:9-14. *"For in Him dwelleth all the fullness of the Godhead bodily. And ye are complete* (perfect, spiritually mature) *in Him, who is the head of all principalities and power; in whom also ye are circumcised with the circumcision made without hands, in putting off the body of the sins of the flesh by the circumcision of Christ; buried with Him in baptism in which ye are risen with Him through the faith of the operation of God, who raised Him from the dead; And you being dead in your sins and the uncircumcision of your flesh hath He made alive together with Him, having forgiven you all trespasses, blotting out the handwriting of ordinance that was against us which was contrary to us , and took it out of the way, nailing it to His cross"* (See also Col. 3:1-11)

By divine infinite power, authority, control, ability, and strength, the Supreme Godhead was fully involved in the resurrection of Jesus Christ. We read in Acts 2:24 that He was raised by God the Father; in Romans 8:11 by God the Holy Spirit; and in

John 10:17-18 that God the Son had the power within Himself to raise Himself up again. (See also Acts 13:34-37 and 1 Pet. 1:18-23) Jesus Christ getting up from the grave, and His resurrection, are an advanced example of the Church, the Body of Jesus Christ. **Webster's Dictionary** defines the word resurrection (anastasis) to mean a return to life, rebirth, renewal, restoration, Christ's rising up from the tomb from the dead, His overcoming of death, His revival and reincarnation. Not only was He wounded for our transgressions and bruised for our iniquities, He was also resurrected for our resurrection (1 Thess. 4:13-18, 1 Pet. 1:3). By His resurrection, every heart that's approved by God shall not be condemned, corrupted, or suffer eternal death (separation from God) (Acts 2:22-23 and 31). None can deny that the resurrection of Jesus Christ was the greatest manifestation (display) of God's almighty power and works in all the earth (Eph. 1:19-23).

God raised Him up on the third day (Acts 10:40), death could not hold Him (Acts 2:24 and 32). He who raised up the Lord Jesus Christ shall also raise us up by Him (2 Cor. 4:14) by His own power (1 Cor. 6:14). If the Spirit of God dwells in us, He shall give life to our mortal bodies by that Spirit in us (Rom. 8:11-13). He was delivered to death for our offenses and was raised again for our justification (we were/are acceptable to God by the death of His Son). He shall die no more, for death has no more dominion over Him (See Rom. 6:4-11). We shall be saved if we confess with our mouths the Lord Jesus Christ and believe in our hearts that God has raised Him from the dead (Rom. 10:9).

Jehovah God raised the dead and has given us life through His risen Son Jesus Christ (Jn. 5:21 and 2 Cor. 1:9). We have been redeemed by the resurrection blood of the Cross of Christ (1 Pet. 1:3 and 18-22). (See also Eph. 1:17-23 and Col. 2:9-13). Saved believers have guaranteed resurrection power only in the Lord Jesus Christ (Jn. 6:39-54). Christ Himself died looking forward by faith unto the day of His resurrection. He spoke of His resurrection: *"He took unto Him the twelve disciples and said unto them, Behold, we go up to Jerusalem and all things that are written by the Prophets concerning the Son of man shall be accomplished. For he shall be delivered unto the Gentiles, and shall be mocked, and spitefully treated and spit on; and they shall scourge Him and put Him to death. And the third day He shall rise again"* (Lk. 18:31-33). (See also Mk. 10:32-34 and Lk. 24:45-48)

"For as Jonah was three days and three nights in the belly of the great

fish, so shall the Son of man be there three days and three nights in the heart of the earth" (Matt. 12:40). (See also Matt. 17:22-23 and Mk. 9:31).

The Cross of Christ was not an execution, but a voluntary act of God for all sin and the salvation of every lost soul. Jesus said this: *"Therefore doth my Father love me, because I lay down my life, that I may take it again. No man taketh it from me, but I lay it down of myself. I have power to lay it down and I have power to take it again"* (Jn. 10:17-18). No man could stop the Lord's beating heart except Himself, and no one could start it again, except God. Death couldn't hold Him, hell couldn't keep Him, and the grave was defeated (Rom. 6:9-10). *"This is my commandment, that you love one another, as I have loved you. Greater love hath no man than this, that a man lay down his life for his friends"* (Jn. 15:12-13). (See also 1 Jn. 3:14-20).

Speaking concerning her brother Lazarus, Martha said: *"Jesus, Lord, if thou had been here, my brother had not* (would not have) *died. Yet I know that even now whatever thou wilt ask of God, God will give it to thee."* Jesus replied: *"Thy brother shall rise again."* Martha said unto Him: *"I know that he shall rise again <u>in the resurrection</u> at the last day."* Jesus said unto her: *"I am the resurrection, and the life; he that believeth in me, though he were dead, yet shall he live. And whosoever liveth and believeth in me shall never die* (not at all, at no time, in no way, and under no circumstances). *Believeth thou this?"*

Martha, from her heart, gave Him her answer that every non-Christian religion, lost sinner, and cult should adhere to. She said unto Him: *"Yea, Lord; I believe that thou art the Christ, the Son of God, who should come into the world"* (Jn. 11:21-27).

The Apostle John was on the isle that is called Patmos for the word of God, and for the testimony of Jesus Christ. Christ said unto him: *"Fear not; I am the first and last; I am He that liveth, and was dead; and, behold, I am alive for evermore, Amen, and have the keys of hell and of death"* (Rev. 1:9-18).

Because of our Lord's victory over death, all true believers not only have "everlasting life," but have passed from death unto life (Jn. 5:24 and 1 Jn. 3:14). No doubt death fought against the resurrection of Jesus Christ, our Champion, but lost the battle and became the last enemy that shall be destroyed (1 Cor. 15:26). This too is great news flowing forth from *The Heart of the Cross.*

The Apostle Paul speaks of the resurrection

God hears the cry of the hearts of His servants. The Apostle Paul, being God's messenger with a message for every ministry, had a fervent love, desire and passion concerning the resurrection of Jesus Christ. He spoke from his heart of His resurrection: *"That I may know Him, and the power of His resurrection, and the fellowship of His suffering being made conformable unto His death, if by any means I might attain unto the resurrection of the dead"* (Phil. 3:10-11). (See also Acts 2:29-32, 4:1-4, 1 Pet. 3:21-22, and Rev. 20:5-14).

"Know ye not that, as many of us as were baptized unto Jesus Christ were baptized unto His death? Therefore, we are buried with Him by baptism into death, that as Christ was raised up from the dead by the glory of the Father, even so we also should walk in the newness of life. For if we have been planted together in the likeness of His death, we shall be also in the likeness of His resurrection; Knowing this, that our old man is crucified with Him, that the body of sin might be destroyed that henceforth we should not serve sin. For he that is dead is freed from sin" (Rom. 6:3-7).

"For when we were yet without strength, in due time Christ died for the ungodly. For scarcely for a righteous man will one die; yet perhaps for a good man some would even dare to die. But God commended His love towards us in that while we were yet sinners, Christ died for us. Much more then, being now justified by His blood, we shall be saved from wrath through Him. For if, when we were enemies (haters of God, foes, opponents, adversaries) *we were reconciled to God by the death of His Son, much more, being reconciled* (reunited), *we shall be saved by His life"* (Rom. 5:6-10). (See also Rom. 4:16-25, 6:9-13, 1 Thess.4:13-18 and 5:9-10)

"For none of us liveth unto himself, and no one dieth to himself. For whether we live, we live unto the Lord; and whether we die, we die unto the Lord; whether we live, therefore or die, we are the Lord's. For to this end Christ both died, and rose and revived, that He might be Lord of both of the dead and living" (Rom. 14:8-9). (See also 1 Cor. 15:1-6 and 2 Cor. 5:14-15).

"For the love of Christ constraineth (restrain, stifle, pressure) *us, because we thus judge that, if one died for all, then were all dead; And that He died for all, that they who live should not henceforth live unto themselves, but unto Him who died for them, and rose again"* (2 Cor. 5:14-15). (See also Acts 10:35-43 and 1 Thess. 4:13-17) Just as He died for all, He also was raised for all.

"But if the Spirit of Him that raised up Jesus from the dead dwell in

you, He that raised up Christ from the dead shall also give life to your mortal bodies by His Spirit that dwelleth in you" (Rom. 8:11). (See also Rom. 4:16-25 and 6:1-9) This is one of our great blessed assurances, and another one equal unto it may be found in Romans 10:9-10, which says: "*If thou shalt confess with thy mouth the Lord Jesus, and believe in thy heart that God has raised Him from the dead, thou shalt be saved. For with the heart man believeth unto righteousness, and with the mouth confession is made unto salvation.*" A believing heart is mandatory. Not only must we confess Christ from our hearts as our Lord and Savior, but also call on and confess His name daily from a pure and clean heart, that we may be saved (Acts 2:21). (See also Acts 10:38-43) He died with all our sins upon Him, but He rose on the third day without sin, having cast our sins as far away from us as the east is from the west (Ps. 103:10-12). Christ died for our sins according to the scriptures, and He was buried, and He rose again the third day according to the scriptures (1 Cor. 15:3-4).

In the midst of Paul's confession, he asks this question: "*How say some of you that there is no resurrection from the dead? If there be no resurrection of the dead then is Christ not risen; then is our preaching in vain and your faith is also vain, and you are yet in your sins. For since by man came death, by man (Christ) also came the resurrection of the dead. For as in Adam all die, even so in Christ shall all be made alive.*" (Study 1 Cor. 15:12-28) So also is the resurrection of the dead. It (our body) is sown in corruption; it is raised in incorruption. It is sown in dishonor; it is raised in glory. It is sown in weakness; it is raised in power. It is sown a natural body; it is raised as a spiritual body. There is a natural body and there is a spiritual body (1 Cor. 15:42-44). The dead in Christ shall be raised incorruptible and we shall be changed. We being corruptible must put on incorruption, and we as mortals must put on immortality; and then shall be brought to pass the saying that is written: Death is swallowed up in victory through our Lord Jesus Christ. (Note 1 Cor. 15:51-58)

By His death, burial, and resurrection we have been given power, authority in the name of Jesus to lay hands on the sick and they are healed by faith, to turn lost sinners from darkness to light, to preach the cross and the gospel of Jesus Christ (Acts 1:8, 26:18, Eph. 1:17-22, 3:20, and 2 Tim. 1:7-8). At the time of life, He shall raise us up by His own power (1 Cor. 6:14). All of these blessings of eternal life and oneness with our Lord forever were made secure by the *Heart of the Cross*, and the resurrection of Jesus Christ.

He Has Risen!

At the end of the Sabbath, as it began to dawn toward the first day of the week, came Mary Magdalene and Mary the mother of James, and others to see the sepulcher. And behold there was a great earthquake for an angel of the Lord descended from Heaven and came and rolled back the stone from the door and sat upon it. His countenance was like lightening and his raiment white as snow. And the angel said unto the women: *"Fear not, For I know that you seek Jesus, who was crucified. He is not here; for He is risen, as He said. Come see the place where the Lord lay. And go quickly, and tell His disciples that He is risen from the dead; and, behold, He goeth before you into Galilee. There shall you see Him"* (Matt 28:5-7) (See Matt. 27:62-66, and Lk. 24:1-12).

Many thousands of people travel to Israel throughout the year to visit Calvary, walking through Gethsemane's garden unto Golgotha's Hill where Jesus was wrongfully crucified and died. Anxiously, their goal is to view the tomb and His sepulcher wherein He was laid. Yet for the past 2,000-plus years, no one has ever seen Him there, for He has risen, just as He said He would.

The facts are in and the case is firmly and forever closed: there is an empty tomb (grave) in Jerusalem! God raised up His Son, the Anointed and Holy One of Israel, the Just (honest, perfect, righteous) Prince of Life, whom God had sent to bless us and turn us from all of our iniquities (Acts 3:15 and 26). *"Blessed be the God and Father of our Lord Jesus Christ, who according to His abundant mercy hath begotten* (brought forth and delivered) *us again unto a living hope by the resurrection of Jesus Christ from the dead to an inheritance incorruptible, and undefiled, and fadeth not away, reserved in Heaven for you"* (1 Pet. 1:3).

Arose (or rise up) means to ascend, mount up, come, or get up; risen means to assume a vertical position after lying down, to surge up after sleeping, resting or death. It may well be said that the Cross of Calvary was mankind at its worst, but the rising of Jesus Christ from the dead was God at His best.

Nine times Jesus appeared to mankind in His resurrected state during the last forty days of His time upon Earth, giving us even greater hope and expectation of eternal life. He chose to go through hell for us so He wouldn't have to go to Heaven without us. He rose up on the third day with all victory and power in His hands, having fulfilled the whole law by a new and living way (Heb. 9:1-26), giving unto His church a new blood covenant that's heart-operated, even a better commandment and testimony. Our pardon, forgiveness, remission, and acquittal of sins are secured forever. Just as we spiritually died with Him, the great news is that we are spiritually risen with Him. He is the one we need. *"For in Him dwelleth all the fullness of the Godhead bodily. And ye are complete* (entire, whole, perfect, no lack, fulfilled, mature) *in Him, who is the head of all principality and power; in whom also ye are circumcised with the circumcision made without hands, in putting off the body of the sins of the flesh by the circumcision* (cutting of the heart) *of Christ; buried with Him in baptism, in which also ye are risen with Him through the faith of the operation of God, who has raised Him from the dead. And you, being dead in your sins and the uncircumcision of your flesh, hath He made alive* (Eph. 2:5) *together with Him, having forgiven you all trespasses* (error, sins, misbehavior, things that offend God) *blotting out the handwriting of ordinances* (laws) *that was again us, which was contrary to us, and took it out of the way, **nailing it to his cross**"* (Col. 2:9-14). He <u>chose</u> the nails. What is it then that we must do?

"*If ye, then, be risen with Christ, seek those things which are above where Christ sitteth on the right hand of God. Set your affection on things above, not on things on the earth. For ye are dead* (to this world and our flesh) *and your life is hidden with Christ in God*" (Col. 3:1-3).

In conclusion, I believe the rising of Jesus Christ was a clear performance of the impossible, showing unto us God's glory and mighty power in open truth and spiritual reality. I believe that between the Cross and the tomb, genetics, genealogy, humanity, and generations came face to face with deity, DNA, God's presence and mighty power. I believe time met with purpose, for the first time the laws of nature met with the laws of physics, and light did taste of the cloaked wrath of darkness and was not defeated. The love of God was stretched far beyond understanding as all sin, sickness, disease, death, and hell hid their faces in preparation to exit. God's will met with His purpose as predestination connected with faith, reality, and truth. Satan and his entire demonic kingdom trembled as "what would be" turned into "that which was already was from the beginning." On the third day, heavenly places revived back to life, eternity was restored back in place, and the grave opened all its gates as the Son of God arose and came forth unto life. He got up and has entered into the hearts of His people and has given unto them a cross to bear. In all of these important things, one of the greatest commandments to be found in the New Testament covenant is now revealed. Come! Take up your cross and follow me! A spiritual cross, not made by the hands of men but by the great hands of God for His precious bride, the Church.

Chapter 5:
The Bearing Of Our Cross

And there went great multitudes with Christ; and He turned and said unto them: *"If any man come to me and hate not his father and mother, and wife, and children, and brethren, and sisters, yes, and his own life also, he cannot be my disciple. And whoever does not <u>bear his cross and come after me</u>, cannot be my disciple"* (Lk. 14:25-27). (See also Matt. 10:37, 16:24, Mk. 8:34-37 and Lk. 9:23-24) Because this saying of Jesus Christ is extremely serious, let us look into the new Living Bible translation of this scripture along with **Webster's Thesaurus Dictionary.** *"If you want to be my disciple* (pupil, learner, follower, believer), *you must hate* (detest, scorn, disapprove, despise, not care for) *anyone else by comparison -- your father and mother, wife and children, brothers and sisters -- and yes even your own life* (to include your existence, being, entity, spirit, breath) *and if you are not willing to do this, you cannot be* (live, endure, continue, abide, prevail, survive as) *my disciple."* Jesus continued to speak to the multitude of people, saying: *"And whoever does not bear* (carry, bring forth, hold up, endure) *his cross and come after me* (move toward, draw near, follow, appear daily) *cannot be my disciple."*

No longer can we afford to neglect or overlook this saying and warning of the Lord concerning our cross, that if we fail to take up <u>our cross</u>, rejection, judgment, and condemnation await us (Matt. 7:21-23). Here the Lord is plainly revealing truth to all who would come (approach, appear, draw near to Him) to be saved: not only must they take up their cross, but must also love Him more than their parents, friends, mates, siblings, riches, their own personal lives, goals, and desires. Considering them all to be far less important than following Christ and serving Him. We must all be willing, if necessary, to let all of them go if it should ever be required to please God and win the Lord Jesus Christ. We must be intimately connected to Him as His body in relationship, be biblically saved, take up our cross and die to sin, self, this world, our flesh, and the works of the devil.

Because our cross is spiritual, we must take hold of it by our spirit (spirit man) through <u>faith</u> (believing, trusting, assurance) by the written, spoken, and living <u>Word</u> of God (word of truth, seed word, God the Word) and <u>love</u> (affection, passion, fondness) of God in the fullness of His grace and tender mercy. This great cross every believing Christian must bear within their hearts is properly revealed and named (*the believer's cross*), one that's not built by the hands of men but by the hands of Yeshua our Messiah and revealed in the gospels (Matt. 10:37-38, Mk. 8:34, and Lk. 9:23). The term <u>take up</u>, according to **Webster's New World Dictionary**, means to begin or start to carry; to commence, grab hold and lift up. To grasp, seize and raise up; to embrace, engage, occupy, escort or to follow, being cross-connected in Christ. To take up our cross exceeds the importance of the Ten Commandments, and is far more beneficial than the Law and Old Testament statutes and judgments. I say this because of the contents and great benefits that lie upon our cross, such as the Word of God, love, faith, new life, the water and blood of Jesus Christ, salvation, His presence, and eternal life, to name a few. While the representation (description) of the word *Cross* signifies pain, suffering, sickness, disease, a curse, sin and separation from God; the expiratory work of Christ on Calvary fulfilled all of these. He expired. Expire means to die, depart, terminate or stop. Christ on Calvary, His death, burial and resurrection, have given our cross a new meaning, one of new life, faith, peace, God's word, love, joy, salvation, the blood of Jesus that we take up daily to follow Him. For many years, due to the lack of revelation knowledge, I believed in error (like most Christians) that our cross and the Cross of Christ were exactly the same, that our cross to bear was one of sin, sickness, suffering, poverty, torment, burdens, or some negative situation that life (or God) had put upon our shoulders to carry. The Holy Spirit revealed that by the Cross of Jesus Christ "*it is finished,*" all works and the powers of darkness were defeated, made null and void, by His stripes we were healed of all sickness and disease, and the penalty and debt of sin and death were all paid in full. Christ is no longer there upon an old rugged cross upon the hill called Calvary, and no longer does He have a cross to bear because He has risen in victory and is there within our hearts as the fullness of our cross within, our spiritual hidden man of the heart, where *The Heart of the Cross* lies today. It may be said like this: *"Upon His cross Jesus carried us, but upon our cross today we carry Him."*

What impacted me the most and inspired me to write this chapter was Matthew 10:37-38, the Lord El Shaddai saying: *"He that loveth father or mother more than me, son or daughter more than me, is not worthy of me. And he that taketh not his cross and follows after me is not worthy of me."* With much concern, I set my heart and with a willing and radical mind, I made this confession unto Him, saying: *"Lord, show me my cross and I will take up my cross daily and follow You."* The first problem I had within me was spiritual ignorance and religious error of understanding that I had been taught to believe by religious and unlearned leaders. I assumed so much and yet knew so little. Like most "religious folks," the only cross I looked to, thought of, or really cared about was the Cross of Jesus Christ; but as you can see, we cannot follow Him, be worthy of Him or be His disciples unless we take up <u>our cross</u> each and every day! As I sat meditating upon this issue (matter of contention), the Lord spoke into my spirit, saying: *"Tell My people that they must come forth, repent of their sins, take hold of Me, love Me, know Me and carry Me, for I am their cross, begotten* (created, formed) *and made from the Tree of Life. I was made a cross for them, just as they were made a cross for Me. My cross led to death so that their cross would be unto peace, joy, love, and life everlasting. They must be believing, obedient, faithful, and they shall be My disciples. If they carry Me* (Word, love, Spirit) *in their hearts, eat and drink of Me daily, they shall live and never die. I am the Lord."*

For many years, I had believed my cross to bear was my trials, sins, afflictions, poverty, lack, misfortune, sickness, or difficulty that came upon a child of God. This simply is not true! Yes, these are weapons Satan uses to attack the body and life of God's people (as well as his own). Our cross <u>in</u> Christ and our faith <u>in</u> the Cross of Christ is our way of escape (Lk. 21:36 and 1 Cor. 10:12-14). Every work Jesus accomplished for us at Calvary was/is finished and the evil works of sin and Satan are of no effect. Jehovah God is not looking upon Calvary where His Son Jesus died, but He looks upon the believer's heart where He lives and is seated upon our cross of the spiritual life, a cross we must bear. Yet in truth we are the Lord's bride, His body, sons and daughters, heirs of the Kingdom, who live in God's heart, as He lives in our hearts; and no weapon formed against us shall prosper. As a singer and a musician, the second issue (challenge) that confronted me was my favorite songs of the cross that I did sing for many years. With joy and gladness, I would perform them upon piano or organ with all my heart. Songs such as *Jesus Keep Me Near The Cross, I Will Cling To The Old Rugged Cross,* and *At The Cross Where I First Saw The Light*, and so on. The writers of these great songs most certainly meant well, and by God's grace have blessed many hearts, lives, and souls. They are all greatly loved and yet very popular. However, upon closer inspection of God's Word of Truth, I found it would have been far better if these songs were properly titled: *Jesus Keep Me Near My Cross, I Will Cling to My Old Rugged Cross,* and *At My Cross is Where I First Saw the Light*. The Cross of Christ stands forever in an "it is finished" position, and we know He is not there! He is no longer there upon that manmade cross and place called Calvary, but He died, was buried, and rose from the tomb (grave) on the third day as He said He would. He lives in us, within our new creature, the very God of our cross is also *The Heart of the Cross*.

It is a sad thing that there has not yet been written songs, sermons, and more teachings about our own cross, so we could see more clearly the purpose, reality, truth and power of both crosses, even the cross of the two thieves. It is a serious matter. Let us take a closer look at what we are religiously asking Him to keep us near, according to most of these songs. We are asking the Lord to keep us near sin, death, sickness, disease, separation from the Father, all condemnation, curses, the power of darkness, pain, sorrow, and all evil that He took upon Himself and died for us on Calvary. Will the Lord keep His people (His precious bride the Church) near the old rugged Cross of Christ? Absolutely not! Even though without the Cross of Christ it would be impossible for anyone to *take up their cross* daily and <u>follow Him</u>. This is because He is the fullness of the cross we must bear. No man then and now could carry the Cross of Jesus Christ spiritually. He desires every believer to take up their own cross of love, faith, God's Word, obedience, new life, the blood of Jesus, and follow Him as His bride, people, the church, His body, and disciples. We are in Christ and are risen with Him (Col. 1:1-4) and are seated with Him in heavenly places (Eph. 2:6). Because our body/heart temple is His dwelling place, we can stay near the Cross of Christ in our hearts, our thoughts, and spirits, living holy and being clothed in our right minds and righteousness. In Luke 9:23-24, Christ spoke to His disciples about their crosses before He went forth to take up His own cross. Apparently He wanted them to set their crosses in order first before Calvary took place, and to be ready to receive their own crosses of blessings and goodness that would flow from His Cross after His resurrection on the third day.

It may well be that in the natural realm on Calvary, it was Jesus being nailed to His cross, but in the spiritual realm it was our cross being nailed to Him. Jesus was giving birth to our cross by the will of God the Father. I believe that as He was being nailed to His cross, all our sins, sicknesses, and iniquities were being nailed to Him. He was being nailed to His Cross by manmade nails, and we by God-made spiritual nails of love, salvation, word, and faith. The more I wrote about the three crosses and the heart of the cross, the more revelation flowed forth and the reason why God looks upon the heart, the place of our cross, that is eternal. Not only is our cross perfect, requiring a perfect heart for all its operations, but it is the perfecting power of our heart (spirit) that we may become perfect in *God's sight*, because Jesus Christ (God's perfect Son) is the presiding Spirit of our cross. His perfect love is there, His perfect Word, Spirit, salvation and will are alive and well within, causing us to increase daily in righteousness, holiness, redemption, justification, sanctification, and truth. For all of this God Himself looks upon the heart (1 Sam. 16:7), our hidden man of the heart (1 Pet. 3:4), the dwelling place of our cross and His only begotten Son. Our holy crosses within our hearts determine our salvation motives, desires, prayer, worship, conversation, thanksgiving, and praises. By His resurrection and His entering into our hearts, we cling to Christ, our spiritual cross, one-on-one, in oneness carrying Him as our cross within our hearts daily in God's presence.

Because we are cross-connected and cross-birthed in Christ, let us view some things that should encourage, motivate, and inspire us to bear our cross.

- We have been raised (lifted, ascended, advanced, increased) with Christ (Matt. 28:1-7, 1 Cor. 15:12-20, Col. 2:12 and 3:1)
- We were all dead in sins, and were without Him (Rom. 6:1-10 and 2 Cor. 5:14-15)
- We were crucified with Christ (Rom. 6:6 and Gal. 2:20)
- We were also buried with Him (Rom. 6:4 and Col. 2:12)
- He dwells in us and we <u>in Him</u> (Jn. 14:20, 15:3-7 and 2 Cor. 5:17)
   - Note: We were chosen in Him before the foundations of this world (Eph. 1:4 and Rev. 13:8)
- Upon His cross He bore our grief and sorrows (Is. 53:4), upon our cross we bear His love, Spirit, Word, blood, joy and peace
- He bore our guilt and shame (Is. 50:6 and Jms. 2:10)
- We have forgiveness of sins (Eph. 4:32, Lk. 23:34, and Col. 1:14)
- We are delivered from the law of sin and death (Gal. 5:1, and Rom. 6:18-22)
- By His stripes we are/were healed (Is. 53:5 and 1 Pet. 2:24)
- We have a new testament and a new covenant by His blood (Matt. 26:28, 1 Cor. 11:25) and a new commandment (Jn. 13:34) (See also Heb. 8:8-13 and 12:24)

- He bore all our sins, transgressions, and iniquities (Is. 53:6-12 and 1 Pet. 2:24)
- We are saved by grace through faith (Jn. 3:16-17 and Eph. 2:5-8)
- Because we are in Christ we are not condemned (Rom. 8:1 and 1 Jn. 3:20-31)

Upon our cross, Christ is not held (stuck, sustained, controlled) by sin or painful nails, but by faith, the nails of God's word that were spiritually driven into the Lamb of God by Agape love in action and power. While both crosses are directly connected, yet there is a difference. The Cross of Christ is still a "new lifeline" for all lost sinners, but our cross is a "new life (lifestyle) and relationship" for all those who are saved. The Cross of Christ was God's responsibility and focus; our cross is our responsibility and focus. Jesus Christ was made a dying sacrifice for sin, separated from God, afflicted and rejected; but when through faith we take up our cross (God's Word and grace) and follow Him, in God's sight, we too are made a living sacrifice unto God; holy, righteous, saved, cleansed, and accepted as sons and daughters. One revelation of the Cross of Christ is the fact that God never intended for sickness, sorrow, sin and death on the Cross of Christ to be more popular in the church than the love, salvation, Word, faith, blood covenant, grace, and new life that rests upon our cross. Jesus shed tears over Jerusalem before He went to the cross (Lk. 19:41), but rejoiced when He looked beyond His cross, saw our cross and Satan defeated (Lk. 10:18-21).

The Lord is extremely visionary (imaginative). No doubt Jesus saw the value of our cross and chose to endure (suffer and survive) His cross. *"Looking unto Jesus, the author and finisher of our faith, who for the joy that was set before Him endured the cross, despising the shame, and is set down at the right hand of the throne of God "* (Heb. 12:2). (See also Mk. 16:19) While most all the teaching and preaching about the Cross of Jesus Christ is valid and true, yet many in error still fail to focus upon their own cross and take it up and follow Him. We must be cross-connected. What makes our cross so important? What gives us the right to take it up in Christ? We are (were) crucified with Christ, we died and are (were) buried with Him, and we are risen with Him.

Viewing some contents of the heart of our cross

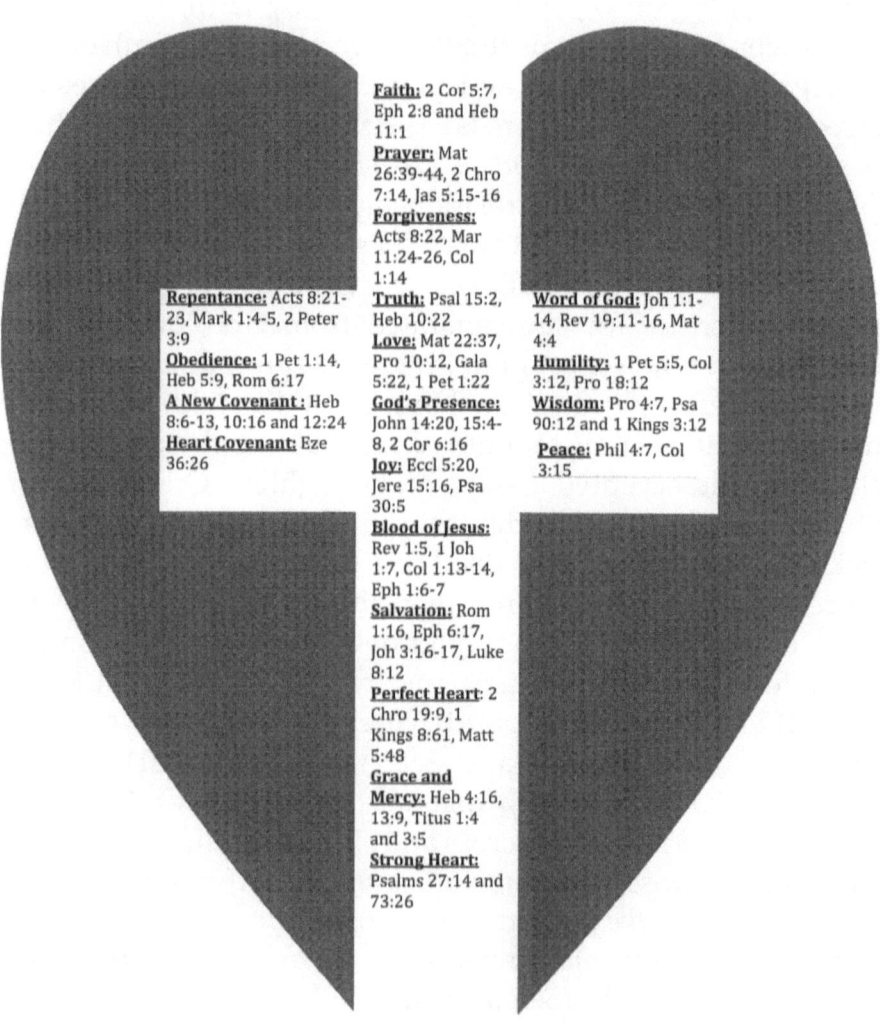

Repentance: Acts 8:21-23, Mark 1:4-5, 2 Peter 3:9
Obedience: 1 Pet 1:14, Heb 5:9, Rom 6:17
A New Covenant: Heb 8:6-13, 10:16 and 12:24
Heart Covenant: Eze 36:26

Faith: 2 Cor 5:7, Eph 2:8 and Heb 11:1
Prayer: Mat 26:39-44, 2 Chro 7:14, Jas 5:15-16
Forgiveness: Acts 8:22, Mar 11:24-26, Col 1:14
Truth: Psal 15:2, Heb 10:22
Love: Mat 22:37, Pro 10:12, Gala 5:22, 1 Pet 1:22
God's Presence: John 14:20, 15:4-8, 2 Cor 6:16
Joy: Eccl 5:20, Jere 15:16, Psa 30:5
Blood of Jesus: Rev 1:5, 1 Joh 1:7, Col 1:13-14, Eph 1:6-7
Salvation: Rom 1:16, Eph 6:17, Joh 3:16-17, Luke 8:12
Perfect Heart: 2 Chro 19:9, 1 Kings 8:61, Matt 5:48
Grace and Mercy: Heb 4:16, 13:9, Titus 1:4 and 3:5
Strong Heart: Psalms 27:14 and 73:26

Word of God: Joh 1:1-14, Rev 19:11-16, Mat 4:4
Humility: 1 Pet 5:5, Col 3:12, Pro 18:12
Wisdom: Pro 4:7, Psa 90:12 and 1 Kings 3:12
Peace: Phil 4:7, Col 3:15

Crucified with Christ

Every true born again believer is *cross-connected with Jesus Christ*. Just as our cross was given birth through the Cross of Christ, we are also crucified with Him. God the Father knew from the beginning that for believers to be *saved* in Christ, they too must have a cross and be crucified with His Son, Jesus Christ. As He went to the cross, we were there in Him (Jn. 14:20, 1 Cor. 8:6) In fact, there are several crucifixions we must partake of as Christians to authenticate our right to carry our cross daily, being crucified and certified as sons of God.

In Galatians 2:20, we need to fully understand what the Apostle Paul was seeking spiritually to reveal unto us concerning the ministry crucifixion. "*I am crucified with Christ: Nevertheless I live; yet not I, but Christ liveth in me; and the life which I now live in the flesh I live by the faith of the Son of God, who loved me and gave himself for me.*" The moment we "take up our cross: we must never seek to lay it down again, because the Lord lives as a permanent resident in the *cross of our heart*. We all were chosen in Christ before creation of this world (Eph. 1:3-5). For this we carry our cross daily and keep our flesh (flesh man) in a crucified position. "*And they that are Christ's have crucified the flesh (works) with the affections and lusts*" (Gal. 5:19 and 24). In this exposition, the word *crucified* means to kill, execute by suffering and persecution. We crucify our old man that our new man may be risen with Christ (Rom. 6:5-6 and Eph. 4:22-24). No one can know their cross and its contents until they truly become crucified with the Lord Jesus Christ, risen with Him, and dwelling in Him (Col. 2:12 and 3:1). The crucifixion of our old man began from the moment we repented (changed directions), turned away from sin (this world system) to God, gave Him our whole heart, life, became born again, and entered into God's Kingdom. In 2 Corinthians 13:4, Christ was crucified through weakness but lived by the power of God. We crucify this world, our flesh, and live by the power of our holy cross and the Cross of Jesus Christ.

Because we were/are in Christ and He is in us (Jn. 14:20, 15:3-7, and 2 Cor. 5:17-21), our cross demands that we all must be crucified with Christ first. Being crucified with Christ we are well able to crucify all wrong such as sexual lusts, immorality, evil thoughts, lying, wicked imaginations, all disobedience, our old sin nature, false doctrine, religion, and the love of money that has become as a plague in all the earth, brought on by leaders who are no less than beggars, money mongrels, schemers, bilchers (as bastards, Deut. 3:2, Heb. 12:8), the servants of mammon (god of money, greed and riches). As servants of mammon, they have yet to realize "The Seed" is the Word of God (Lk. 8:11). Because they operate their money ministry by the spirit of mammon (Matt. 6:24). They fail to teach it is the seed word of God and not money that gives us strength to crucify our old corrupt man (nature), helping us to put on our new man (new nature) to be crucified with Christ, and to carry our cross. *"That ye put off (crucify) concerning the former manner of life the old man which is corrupt according to the deceitful lusts, and that you put on the new man, which after God is created in righteousness and true holiness"* (Eph. 4:22-24). (See also 1 Tim. 3:4-5 and Col. 3:9-10)

When we were baptized into Jesus Christ, we were baptized into His death and buried with Him, that by His resurrection we are able to walk in the newness of life (new heart, right mind, new covenant, and direction), knowing our old man is crucified with Him, that the body of sin might be destroyed and from this day on (henceforth) we should not serve sin (Rom. 6:3-8). In Galatians 6:14, the Apostle Paul identifies a double crucifixion we all should partake of if we expect to carry our cross unto the end. *"But God forbid that I should glory, except in the cross of our Lord Jesus Christ; by whom <u>the world is crucified unto me and I unto the world</u>."* This means this world is a dead, sinful place for us, having no life in it that's eternal. It causes its victims to have a "far away heart" that has no strength to carry a cross in Christ (Is. 29:13 and Mk. 7:5-8). A distant heart has caused many to be lost in this world, lost in the House of God, having many Sunday services without God's presence. The Apostle Paul, as God's heart of the cross messenger, was given a great message for every soul-winning ministry, which is <u>first of all</u> Jesus Christ and Him crucified. In 1 Corinthians 2:1-2, he said this: *"And I brethren, when I came to you, I came not with excellency of speech or of wisdom, declaring unto you the testimony of God. For I determined not to know anything among you, except Jesus Christ, and him crucified."* We must pray daily that the Holy Spirit will be able to give birth to every church the mandatory crucifixion message of every believer and the importance of the cross message and ministry, far above riches, money, and cares of this world.

Do not think for a moment that our old sinful flesh man wants to be crucified with Christ. We can expect to have a battle in our minds and much warfare in our hearts. As lost sinners we were dead in trespasses and sins (Eph. 2:1), by Christ's death, burial, and resurrection we are/were made alive, became dead to sin, and now we rest safe and secure with Christ <u>in</u> God. We become dead to sin and eternal death with Christ (Col. 2:13-20, 3:1-4, and 2 Cor. 5:14), we have His shed blood for the remission of sins (Matt. 26:28 and Heb. 9:22). We live securely by the forgiveness of sins (Eph. 1:17 and Col. 1:14), because He became sin for us. We have received the fullness of Jesus into our hearts and we have direct access to the fullness of our cross and His cross as well. It is all about a crucified heart (spirit) that gives us power to live a crucified life. We have the access code, the Holy Spirit (Eph. 2:15-18), wherein we are counted as saved sons and daughters and no longer lost sinners.

In Galatians 5:22, we can see clearly that the Fruit of the Spirit is found in abundance upon our cross: *"But the fruit of the Spirit is love, joy, peace, long-suffering* (patience), *gentleness, goodness, faith, meekness, self-control* (temperance)," and in verse 24; "*they that are Christ's have crucified the flesh with the affections and lusts.*" The power of our spiritual crucifixion comes by the love of God through the shed blood of Jesus, our faith in God, salvation, new birth, the Living Word, a new heart, and a new, sound mind. Wisdom reveals that Christ was nailed to His cross by our sins and crucified by the hands of hateful evil men (Acts 2:22-24). As of this day, I am still seeking to know more about the terminology of His cross and my cross, which is <u>personal</u>, our cross and their cross, which is <u>collectively</u>, and your cross, which is <u>objectively</u>. I do know that in this both God and man are heart-connected. If we should look deep into *The Heart of the Cross* of Jesus Christ, we are there, and if we should look deep into the heart of our cross, He is there. I say this to those who stand in a leadership position, that they be teachable and realize the Cross of Jesus is/was made by the hands of men and cannot always be compared to our cross, which is made by the hands of God. All things of value were in Christ, who made all things (Jn. 1:1-14).

In biblical times when they crucified someone, the sins and offenses of the guilty victims were written upon their crosses. But upon the Cross of Jesus Christ a superscription was written in Greek, Latin, and Hebrew: "*This is the King of the Jews*" (Lk. 23:38). This was God's doing because He knew no sin and had done no wrong. What then should be written upon our cross of crucifixion? This is God's child, a son and lover of God, a believer, Christian, the Lamb's bride, the Church, and the body of Jesus Christ.

As we put on the Lord Jesus Christ as our spiritual covering (Rom. 13:14), and put on the whole armor of God (Eph. 6:10-18), being Spirit-filled (Acts 2:1-4), washed in the blood of the Lamb of God (Rev. 1:5), walking in love, faith and godliness; having our names written in the Lamb's Book of Life, we are well able to perform one of the greatest acts upon the earth. This is to <u>deny ourselves</u>, take up our crosses and follow Jesus Christ, the God of our salvation, who is the fullness of our crosses within our hearts.

Deny Yourself, Take Up Your Cross and Follow Me

In Luke 9:23, the Apostle Luke, the physician, records the words of Jesus concerning the serious matter of our cross and following the Lord. *"If any man will COME* (draw near, move toward, come along) *after me, let him DENY* (give up himself, refuse, forget self-desires, disallow, disown himself, not acknowledge or recognize) *himself and TAKE UP* (lift, begin, raise, occupy, use) *his cross DAILY* (everyday, day in and day out, day after day) *and FOLLOW* (pursue, chase, mirror, be an example of) *Me."* (See also Matt. 16:24) It is very clear that the Lord wants every believer on earth to come to Him, approach Him, take up their cross to follow Him and discover more and more of Him. It doesn't require money, fame, or perfection but a repentant heart, a given life, a changed renewed mind, a will to hear and obey His voice, and to cleave steadfastly to Him. As we take up our cross of glory, grace, love, faith, blood, salvation and eternal life, we deny and let go of our old sinful lifestyle, our *old man*, and lost heart that was leading us unto eternal condemnation, and come to Jesus just as we are. It is free, there is no charge; the price has already been paid.

Now here is the issue (problem, matter) of anyone coming to Jesus Christ and the reason why they must <u>deny</u> themselves. After repentance, newborn believers must go through a season of self-denial, denying themselves of open sin and this world's goods. Wanting worldly pleasures, ungodly desires, fleshly lusts, temptations, carnality, having an "I, me, my, and mine" self-centered attitude. There will be inner struggles, heart wars, and battles of the mind, body, and soul. Yet self-denial is mandatory, otherwise they will become heavy laden with self-desire, needs, wanting, greed, and overall self-focused. Our new lives in the crossways of salvation are not based upon ourselves, such as self-willed, self-righteous, self-centered, and the evil pride of self-blessed. In Luke 9:24-25, the Lord makes it more clear and plain, saying: *"For whosoever would save his life* (refusing to carry his cross) *shall lose it, but whosoever will lose his life for my sake* (and take up his cross given by My hands and life) *the same shall save it. For what good* (or profit) *is it if a man gain the whole world and lose his own soul?* (Be rejected of God on Judgment Day)" (See also Matt. 7:21-23 and Rev. 20:12-15)

Webster's Thesaurus Dictionary further defines the word "deny" to mean to withhold from, disallow, refuse to acknowledge, placing God's will, desires and cares above our will, desires, and cares. All lost sinners do deny the Lord in various ways, but not themselves (Tit. 1:16 and 2 Pet. 2:1). It is a shame, even a travesty when we come to the Lord, touch Him, know Him, and in times of trouble, sickness, temptation, or woe, deny Him. *"If we suffer, we shall also reign with Him; if we deny Him, He will also deny us; If we believe not, yet He abideth faithful: He cannot deny Himself"* (2 Tim. 2:12-13). (See also Gal. 5:16-17, 2 Thess. 1:5, 1 Tim. 4:10, 1 Pet. 2:20 and 3:14-17) Because of our cross and His presence in our hearts, we do none of the evil works we used to do as lost sinners. We cannot do the things we would because we have been bought with the price of the Cross of Jesus Christ (1 Cor. 6:20 and 7:23) and the heart of our cross of spiritual life is ever before us. We are to deny ourselves of all ungodliness (Tit. 2:11-12). We deny our sinful nature, our fleshly self-person because they are not eternal. Denying ourselves the things of this world must be our daily desire, focus, and lifestyle. Though we may suffer loss of money, friends, loved ones, suffer sickness or disease, and broken relationships, we have the victory and power through the crosses we bear within us. Yet in these last days, there are those who simply refuse to take up their cross of godliness and deny themselves, for they love their religion more than righteousness, money and riches more than a godly relationship. They refuse to deny themselves their fleshly desires, evil lusts, the love of money, illegal sex, and the deceitful works of darkness. These have a form of godliness, knowledge of the right way, yet their hearts are far away from the Lord (Mk. 7:6-8). They profess that they know God, but in works they deny Him, being abominable, disobedient, and unto every good work reprobate (Tit. 1:16). (See also Matt. 10:32-33, 16:24, and Mk. 8:34)

Most have been deceived by false religion, traditions, and

doctrines of men that have a form of godliness, who deny the presence and power of God in their Sunday services (2 Tim. 3:5 and Jude 4). God will deny them on Judgment Day (Matt. 7:21-23). "*This know, also, that in the last days perilous times shall come. For men shall be lovers of their own selves* (Rom. 1:21-23) *covetous, boasters, proud, blasphemers, disobedient to parents, unthankful, unholy; without natural affection, trucebreakers, false accusers, incontinent, fierce, despisers of those that are good traitors, high minded, lovers of pleasures more than lovers of God, having a form of godliness, but <u>denying</u> the power of it; from such turn away*" (2 Tim. 3:1-5). Far too many look holy, righteous, and pure in public, but not in private behind closed doors. Many enter the church doors on Sunday while their hearts and minds are still at home on the Internet or watching TV, denying fellowship and service unto God. In Matthew 26:34-35 and 60-75, we read how Peter in his flesh denied the Lord three times. Like most of us, he looked upon the surrounding circumstances and chose to lie and deny the Lord who had earlier told Peter exactly what he would do. By no means do I tend to imply that we shall not need to war, fight, suffer heavy burdens, have some valleys to cross, make mistakes, endure dark and cloudy days, have mountains and hills to climb, woes and tear-stained sleepless nights. We shall have distress and trouble (Rom. 8:34-39 and 2 Cor. 4:8-10), some tribulations (Acts 14:22), sickness and disease, but none of these things shall have the power to rule over us, so long as we do not deny our faith in the Cross of Jesus Christ or neglect to take up our cross and follow Him.

The burdens we often carry are for the care of our family, lost loved ones, their issues, illnesses, needs and woes. We become intercessors unto God, crying tears for our pastors, and children who have been caught in Satan's web of evil, sin, worldly cares, riches, and wrongdoing. God is never in a hurry (we can't hurry God), yet He is concerned and He sits in an "*it is finished*" position with outstretched arms, speaking unto heavy, hurting, lonely and broken hearts from eight "me" concepts:

1. Deny yourself and come unto <u>Me</u>
2. Know <u>Me</u>
3. Love <u>Me</u>
4. Walk with <u>Me</u>
5. Follow <u>Me</u>
6. Have faith in <u>Me</u>

7. Dwell in <u>Me</u> (Jn. 15:3-7)
8. Serve <u>Me</u>

Our great concern, as well as the Lord's, is this: our heart has the power to turn from God (Deut. 29:18, Is. 44:20, Acts 7:39) and to depart from Him (Jer. 17:5 and Heb. 3:12) without our permission. For this our *Yes* to God is great, we deny ourselves, giving ourselves to prayer without ceasing, to walk in the love of God from our hearts through faith and not by sight; having this attitude: "wherever He leads me, I will follow." To deny ourselves also means to die to self, flee from selfishness and personal viewpoints that don't give God the glory and honor, and will hinder us from walking in His presence and approval. Self-denial is made easy when we set our hearts, minds, and souls to obey God's word and to do His will.

Far too many believers wear a cross of Jesus Christ around their necks or upon their clothes and fail to carry their own crosses within their hearts. This may be listed as a great heart failure event of spiritual life, even a spiritual heart attack. As we live a denied worldly lifestyle, we must keep our eyes, hearts, and minds stayed on the Lord: "*Looking unto Jesus, the author and finisher of our faith, who for the joy that was set before Him endured the cross, despising the shame, and sat down at the right hand of the throne of God*" (Heb. 12:2). Let us ever be mindful that on Calvary, man was at his worst, but God was at His best.

A simple prayer to start our day

Lord, give me a mouth to speak Your words, a mind to do and obey Your will, a strong heart and mind to carry my cross, as I deny myself today and follow You.

Let me be victorious over my flesh, will, evil lust and desires, thoughts, imaginations and Satan's evil web of temptation, love of money, lusts and wrong thinking, that I may say at the close of every day, it is well with my soul.

We must never deny ourselves morning prayer, for it is well spoken that a day hemmed in prayer will never unravel. Denying ourselves, along with obedience, is both a commandment, an instruction, and is the perfect will of God. It keeps us from the quagmire of selfishness; living for self through radical self-denial. We place all of Satan's evil plans for us on hold. When we deny ourselves from our hearts, there are great benefits we will enjoy. As the bride of Christ, we will not be walking behind Him but <u>beside Him</u>. As our husband (Jn. 15:1 and Jms. 5:7), should we ever stumble and fall, He will lift us up and carry us for a time or season. He is our great God, Savior, and Husbandman.

There came a day in my life when I bowed down upon my knees, and looking up to Heaven, I began to pray earnestly about a serious situation I was going through. As I looked up to the hills, where I believed my help came from, I heard a still small voice say unto me; *"Why are you looking up to Heaven and the hills when you pray? Don't you know that I am <u>in</u> you, in your heart? My son, your heart is My dwelling place!"*

Immediately, I looked upon my own heart and began to worship, pray, give thanks and rejoice, having the revelation that I carry Him within my heart daily, just as He carries me within His heart. As we follow Him, we also live and walk <u>in</u> Him and He lives and walks <u>in</u> our hearts. (See Jn. 14:20, 15:4-7, 17:21 and 2 Cor. 6:16-17) As we follow Him, our cross is rooted and manifested <u>in</u> Him and the Cross of Christ is manifested <u>in</u> us. Spiritually speaking, both crosses are as one in God, and He is working through us, in us, for us, and with us as we follow and work in Him, through Him and for Him. The first step is to <u>come to Him</u>, to be washed from sin, cleansed, restored, redeemed, filled with His Spirit and a new heart.

With an open heart, arms open wide, and with a loud voice, the Lord calls out unto all nations and people, saying: "<u>*Come unto me*</u>*, all ye that labor and are heavy laden, and I will give you rest. Take my yoke* (bonding, servitude, burden) *upon you, and learn of me; for I am meek and lowly in heart and you shall find rest unto your souls, for my yoke is easy and my burden is light"* (Matt. 11:28-30). (See also Is. 48:16-18 and Mk. 1:17) Not all who come to the Lord is willing to follow Him wherever He may lead. This is because many are religious and follow men and have yet to take up their crosses. In John 7:37, the Lord again cried out, saying: *"If any man thirst let him come to me and drink."* Carrying our crosses daily keeps us hungry for His presence, and thirsty for more of His righteousness and salvation.

"Come, everyone that thirsteth, come to the waters, and he that has no money, come, buy and eat; yea, come, buy wine and milk without money and without price. Incline your ear, and <u>come unto me</u>; hear, and your soul shall live" (Is. 55:1-3 and Joel 3:18). Coming to God also means we are going to God from a place and position we no longer desire to be. We

were all dead in our trespasses and sins (Eph. 2:1). Some have come to Jesus wounded, some running from the devil, sick, beaten, infected by this world, and having Satan hot on their trail. *Come* is the basic revelation of the gospel. To come to Christ is a conscious heart decision, but to come after Him (follow Him) is a way of a committed life. It requires a given heart, our willingness to deny ourselves, along with a made-up mind. The Lord calls all of His sheep to Him, that they may deny themselves their own fleshly desires and ungodliness, take up their crosses and come after Him. When we come to Christ, and then come after Him, we must never be found looking back to turn from Him in our hearts and to go back into a world of sin. "*And Jesus said unto him, No man, having put his hand to the plough, and looking back is fit for the Kingdom of God*" (Lk. 9:59-62). The Prophet Elijah saw this "looking back" spirit in the children of Israel and said this: "*How long shalt ye halt* (stand, stop) *between two opinions? If the Lord be God, follow Him; but if Baal* (god of the Canaanites, Satan in disguise) *then follow him*" (1 Kgs. 18:21). (See my book, *The Power of Opinion*.) We are to come out of this world and be separated (2 Cor. 6:17 and Rev. 18:4). He is able to save to the utmost (maximum, full, most, total, complete) those who come to God (Heb. 7:25). We are to come to the Lord to be healed (Lk. 13:14). We must come to Him, not as adults but as children (Matt. 18:1-6). We do not come in our own names, but in the precious name of Jesus (Jn. 14:13-14 and Acts 3:6). Neither must we come to Him in our flesh but in the spirit and in truth, expecting to know Him, touch Him, and to worship at His feet and drink of the water of His presence, even the blood of His Cross.

For the backslider in heart and lost sinner, there is great news: if they will return to the river of God's glory and walk upon the shores of repentance, love, and the grace of God, and follow Him, He will literally come to them. "*Come, and let us return unto the Lord; for He has torn and He will heal us, He has smitten, and He will bind us up. After two days He will revive us; in the third day He will raise us up and we shall live in His sight. Then shall we know if we follow on to know the Lord; His going forth is prepared as the morning and* He shall come unto us *as the rain, as the latter and former rain unto the earth*" (Hos. 6:1-3). (See also Lk. 19:13 and Jn. 10:10)

Both sinning backsliders and the front-sliding believers must come unto His presence that He may rain righteous upon them for this great promise of Christ. "*All that the Father giveth me shall come to* me; and him that cometh to me I will in no wise cast out" (Jn. 6:37) (See also Jn. 6:44-65) All who come to Him must take up their cross daily and follow after Him, seek and search for Him to find, and touch Him even though He is never far away from any one of us (Acts 17:27). Our Lord sticks closer to us than a brother (Pr. 18:24). We must make daily contact with Him. "*And the Spirit and the bride say, COME. And let him that heareth say, COME and let him that thirst COME. And whoever will, let him take the water of life freely*" (Rev. 22:17).

Let us remember that our spiritual heart is the only element in the earth that has the power and contents to follow the Lord. It has the power to travel at the speed of thought, move slowly as a snail or turtle, or stand still and be unmovable. "*A man's heart, directeth (plans, invents, regulates) his way, but the Lord directeth His steps*" (Pr. 16:9). And again in 2 Thessalonians 3:5; "*And the Lord direct your hearts into the love of God, and into the patient waiting for Christ.*" (See also Pr. 3:6) The Lord is both our life and heart director. We shall never be found going in the wrong direction. As we deny ourselves, take up our crosses, and increase our faith in the Cross of Jesus Christ, we become more effective as God's people and established as true followers of Jesus Christ.

I would like to narrate a few scriptures of Mark, the author of the book of Mark, who recorded a serious conversation between Jesus Christ and a rich young ruler, who came to Him, saying: "*Good Master, what shall I do that I may inherit eternal life? Then Jesus beholding him, loved him, and said unto him; One thing thou lackest, go thy way, sell whatever thou has and give to the poor, and thou shall have treasure in Heaven; and come, take up the cross (your cross) and follow me*" (Mk. 10:17-21). The rich young ruler became sad at the sayings of Christ and went away, grieved, for he had great possessions. Because his eyes and heart were blinded by his great wealth, he could not see or identify the spiritual riches that Christ was offering him, and that to take up his cross was far greater treasure than all the material riches the young ruler possessed, especially the riches of the Cross of Christ and eternal life being offered unto him. The Lord revealed that taking up our crosses and following Him by the grace of the Cross of Christ was far greater wealth than all earthly riches and treasures, known and unknown. Sadly, like some of us, the rich young ruler didn't have the heart and mind to deny himself (leave self behind, disregard, give up all rights to himself to God) to come to the Lord and take up his cross and follow Christ by faith. By this we see that if we wish to be saved, we must walk with Christ, carry our crosses, follow Him, and be willing to revoke, rebut, and dismiss all personal worldly cares, wealth, goals and desires of this life, especially those of our flesh.

Jesus turned and spoke to His disciples, saying: *"How hardly* (with what difficulty) *shall they that have riches enter into the Kingdom of God;"* thus indicating that our cross, its contents, and our following are the key to our entering into God's Kingdom, and eternal life.

The State of Our Heart and Cross in a Sin-Free Position

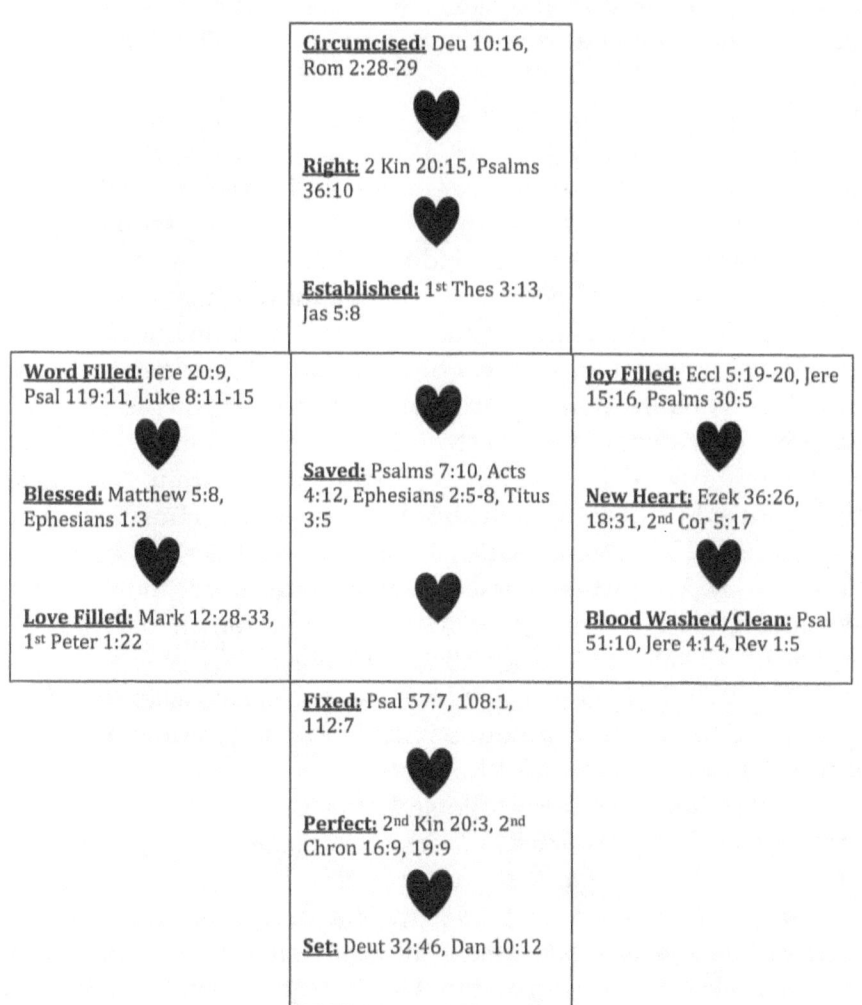

Follow Me

Our God is a jealous God. We must love Him and follow Him above all else. In Matthew 10:38, Jesus Christ Adonai said this: "*He that loveth father or mother more than me is not worthy of me; and he that loveth son or daughter more than me, is not worthy of me. And he that <u>taketh not his cross</u> and followeth after me, is not worthy of me.*"

The living and saved believer will embrace their cross to follow Christ, but the living dead will not. Not only are all those who refuse to follow Him considered as dead (breathless) while they yet live, but are as spiritual churchologists, religious, hypocrites, unclean, ungodly, and in secret are enemies of Jesus Christ (Phil. 3:18-19). We must be mindful that without a cross to bear, not only are we unworthy (dishonorable, offensive and unfit), but we can never follow Christ and be His disciples. Without our crosses of faith, love, word, blood, and grace, we have no strength, energy, or desire to follow Him. As followers, we are "sheep" of God's pasture. Sheep must have a shepherd. Among all four-legged creatures on the Earth, sheep are the least intelligent. They do not know where to go, and if they should leave the shepherd and flock, they seldom find their way back. They know not what to eat or drink, and if they get into deep water they will immediately perish, not being able to swim. They are easy prey for wolves of the forest; and those in the church who wear fine clothes outwardly while having lustful hearts within. As long as Israel followed Jehovah Elohim and didn't turn from Him, they were blessed (Josh. 22:16-29). (See also 1 Sam. 12:14-20, 1 Kgs. 9:1, and 2 Chron. 34:33). When they ceased to follow the Lord, they became losers and not winners. It is good to reiterate and remember what the Prophet Elijah said in 1 Kings 18:21: "*How long halt ye between two opinions? If the Lord be God, follow Him; but if Baal, then follow him.*" By this we shall follow the Lord our Savior or Satan the sinner. (See also Num. 32:11-12, Jdg. 2:19 and 1 Kgs. 9:6-7)

The Prophet Isaiah also followed after God and gave us these instructions, saying: "*Hearken unto me, ye that follow after righteousness, ye that seek the Lord; look unto the rock from which ye are hewn, and to the hole of the pit from which ye are digged*" (Is. 51:1). "*Blessed is he that hunger and thirst after righteousness, for they shall be filled*" (Matt. 5:6). Religion makes us religious, but God's righteousness makes us righteous and holy. Christ was made the righteousness of God unto us (1 Cor. 1:30), that we may be made the righteousness of God in Christ (2 Cor. 5:21). Righteousness defined means someone who is godly, honest, virtuous, holy, just, upright in heart, and devoted to a sinless life. In John 12:16, Jesus said this: *"If any man serve me, let him follow me; and where I am, there shall my servant be; if any man serve me, him will my Father honor"* (Jn. 12:26). In righteousness, our cross is plainly visible, in holiness the Lord is clearly seen. We confess Jesus Christ as true Christians, saying: He is our shepherd (Ps. 23) and we are the sheep of His pasture (Ps. 79:13 and 95:7), who daily follow after Immanuel our Messiah. His arms are open wide and His voice still speaks unto all nations from on high, saying: *"Come, take up your cross and follow me!"* Let us be reminded that the word *follow* further means to come after, conform to, observe, imitate, follow the Lord's example and obey.

Life is a journey, and as God's sheep we spiritually follow Christ from our hearts and are known as "followers of God." The state of our hearts and the condition of our minds determine our footsteps. Having (keeping) a right mind and pure heart assures us we are good followers and blessed (empowered to prosper) with great benefits. Warning! Beware! Imperfect people cannot (will not) follow a perfect God. A perfect heart is mandatory (required). As we follow Him, we must always be aware and mindful of who or what is following us. If we refuse to follow Christ, Satan, hell, and all evil will surely follow us. As we take up our crosses and follow, we learn more about what our crosses are and all they represent. As cross-bearers and new creatures in Christ, we become love, word, righteousness, faith, holiness unto God, in truth and likeness. We are continually changed by the contents of our crosses in our hearts, transformed into His likeness and image as sons of God. We cannot receive the full blessings and benefits of our cross-bearing without a firm commitment to follow Him daily and obey. After His resurrection, three times Jesus went to Peter, saying: *"Feed my sheep,"* and His final words unto him were *"follow me"* (Jn. 21:19-22).

In Matthew 4:19, He told Peter and his brother, Andrew: *"Follow me and I will make you fishers of men."* David followed God with all his heart (1 Kgs. 14:8). Somehow David knew his heart was the only power on earth that was able to do God's will, obey His commandments, and to follow Him. We give the Lord our whole heart, holding nothing back, knowing the contents of our crosses are heart-operated. In Matthew 8:22, one of His disciples said to Jesus:

"*Lord, suffer* (permit) *me first to go and bury my father.*" But Jesus said unto him: "*Follow me, and let the dead bury their dead.*" He opened the disciple's eyes to the fact that there are those in the Earth who are alive and living but are yet dead; persons who have never came alive in Christ to take up their own crosses, but are yet devoted to a sinful and hellish life.

In John 10:3-5, we are the sheep of His pasture; we hear His voice, we are led by Him, and we will not follow the voices of strangers, but will flee from them. (See also Matt. 5:14 and Jn. 8:12) "*He that followeth after righteousness and mercy findeth life, righteousness and honor*" (Pr. 21:21). With holy boldness, a radical mindset and attitude, we speak unto all others with a loud, clear voice, saying: "*Wherever He leads me, I will follow!*" As we carry our crosses in our hearts and follow the Lord, we keep our minds and hearts stayed on Him. Here are some theological concepts of the word *follow*:

- **Who do we follow?** We follow El Shaddai, the Lord Jesus Christ
- **Why do we follow?** He gives us an expected ending wherein we are kept from death, hell, and the grave. He alone is the way, the truth, and the life.
- **What do we follow?** We follow His word, voice, and gentle instructions, His righteousness and truth.
- **When do we follow?** From the hour of salvation and repentance. The moment He says, "*Come, follow me.*"
- **Where do we follow?** In the waters, in the sanctuary, wherever He leads.
- **How do we follow?** By faith and obedience to His word, His commandments, the laws of love, and hearing His voice.

Let us view some important concepts of following Jesus Christ as we carry our precious, powerful, and priceless crosses.
- The more we take up our crosses daily and follow the Lord, we come to know Him (Phil. 3:10-14), we hear His voice (Jn. 10:27), and come to know who we are. The gospel, salvation, and benefits of eternal life are predicated upon our cross-bearing and following Him.
- Even though a true church may teach the gospel of the Cross of Jesus Christ, it is useless and ineffective if believers refuse to go on unto Yeshua and enter into a love relationship,

knowing His will, who He is, and who they are <u>in</u> Him.
- Following God is a personal choice, a heart and mind decision. As we follow Him, we can expect to see and experience miracles, blessings, and joy in His presence. Our character shall match our call of God, our message and works will fulfill the measure and expectation of our spiritual life.
- Following Christ is also a New Testament commandment (Matt. 4:19-21 and 9:9). As He walked upon the Earth, multitudes did follow Him (Matt. 8:1-19). We are to follow after righteousness. He is our righteousness (1 Tim. 6:11 and 2 Tim. 2:22). Righteousness (godliness, virtuous and piety) exhalts a nation.
- He is our peace and we are to follow after peace (Heb. 12:14). We are to follow the steps of Jesus Christ the Lamb of God (1 Pet. 2:21 and Rev. 14:14).
- Christ our Messiah spoke of great benefits that await all who follow Him. Then Jesus spoke again unto them, saying; *"I am the light of the world, he that followeth me shall not walk in darkness, but shall have the light of life"* (Jn. 8:12). (See also Matt. 5:14)
- Our works do follow us (Rev. 14:13). We must follow the Lord as sheep follows their shepherd (Jn. 1:4-27). We shall have great treasure (benefits, wealth) in Heaven if we go on to follow the Lord (Lk. 18:22). We must be willing to forsake all to follow El Shaddai (Lk. 5:11). We must follow after righteousness by faith (Rom. 9:30-31).
- The Prophet Jeremiah also followed God (Jer. 17:16). Jehovah loves those who follow after righteousness (Pr. 15:9). We are commanded in 2 Timothy 2:2 to *"flee youthful lusts, and follow righteousness, faith, love, and peace with them that call on the Lord out of a <u>pure heart</u>."* (See also Pr. 15:9, 21:21, Rom. 9:30, 1 Tim. 6:11 and Heb. 12:14).
- We must *stretch* ourselves, yield our bodies daily to obedience and proceed forth in spite of our faults, weakness, sins, and frailties, and follow in the footsteps of Jesus Christ (1 Pet. 2:21 and Rev. 14:4). With new spiritual hands, feet, minds and a new heart, we take hold of our crosses daily and follow Christ. The closer we follow Him, the greater our flow of spiritual life will be. Must we always follow behind Him?

Most assuredly not! Because we are His children, sons and daughters, often we will find ourselves walking beside Him as His friend, His bride, and His body.
- The moment we take up our crosses and follow Christ, we grow to become more like Him, willing to do His will, and have the power to do His works (Jn. 14:12). For all of these things our crosses are extremely serious.

In fact, our crosses stand as a spiritual mark and identification of who and whose we really are. I say again that all, regardless of race, creed, or color, who refuse to take it up and follow Christ are as enemies of the Cross of Christ (Phil. 3:10-18). From the moment we take hold of our cross through faith, we begin to change and become more of what our great cross truly is. We become praise, worship, word-filled, righteousness, love, sons of God, His friends, God's temple, His likeness and image in the earth. We become cross-connected and cross over from death unto life and from finite to infinite as His church and body.

The Old Testament covenant to follow God was physical, of the flesh, but by a new covenant of the cross of Jesus Christ, it is spiritual, infinite, of the Holy Spirit. In every case "follow" is an action (active) word. After repentance, *"follow me"* is one of the most important commandments from God to all believers. Victory is determined by the contents of our cross. We do not seek and follow Him in our flesh of humanity and carnality, but in the spirit and in truth from our hearts (Jn. 4:23-24 and Gal. 5:15-16). In John 6:48-69, many came to Yeshua and followed Him until He spoke of their eating of His flesh (partaking of His body) and drinking of His blood (receiving the blood of His cross). They walked no more with Him, including many of His disciples. *"From that time, many of His disciples went back and walked no more with Him"* (Jn. 6:1-2 and 66). Because the four Gospels were still under Old Testament law, followers of God walk with Jesus Christ. After the Cross, they would walk in Christ and He in them and dwell in them (2 Cor. 6:16-18). Jesus Christ is our Chief Cornerstone, the rock of our salvation, the Stone of Israel that followed Israel through the wilderness. They ate of manna and drank water from "The Rock," the Chief Cornerstone that was Christ. *"And did all drink the same spiritual drink; for they drank of that spiritual rock that followed them and that rock was Christ"* (1 Cor. 10:1-4). Here we see a revelation that the Lord followed Israel, but Israel did not follow

Chapter 5: The Bearing Of Our Cross

after the Lord as He had commanded.

As we take up our crosses and follow Christ, some signs will be following us. And these signs <u>shall follow</u> those who believe: *"In my name shall they cast our demons, they shall speak with new tongues; they shall take up serpents; and if they drink any deadly thing, it shall not hurt them; they shall lay hands on the sick and they shall recover"* (Mk. 16:17-20). By the taking up of our crosses we shall see clearly who we are following, who or what is following us, and if there is anything following us that we need to get rid of.

David confessed in Psalm 23:6 that God's goodness and mercy would follow him all the days of his life. Jehovah Elohim Himself states that David, His servant, kept His commandments and followed Him with all of his heart, doing what was right in His sight (2 Kings 14:8). (See also 1 Sam. 12:14-20 and Ps. 63:8) We must not follow false teachers (2 Pet. 2:1-2) or waterless and spiritless (want-to-be) leaders who do not have the Spirit of Christ and have no true knowledge of the right way (Lk. 17:22). (See also Rom. 8:9) These are the blind who lead the blind.

In Proverbs 21:21, wisdom speaks loud and clear, saying: *"He that followeth after righteousness and mercy findeth life, righteousness and honor."* We also follow after love (1 Cor. 14:1). I pray all believers see how serious the taking up of our cross to follow Christ is. In 1 Corinthians 4:16, the Apostle Paul instructs the church, saying: *"Wherefore, I beseech you, be ye followers of me,"* and again in 1 Corinthians 11:1: *"Be ye followers of me, even as I also am of Christ."* In writing to the Ephesian church, he affirms our following: *"Be ye, therefore, followers of God, as dear children; and walk in love as Christ has also loved us"* (Eph. 5:1). (See also 1 Thess.1:5-6, Heb. 6:11-12 and 1 Pet. 3:13-16) Just as our coming to Christ was a heart decision, a mindset and a soul desire, so it is with our crosses.

As we follow the Lord, we must not look for material gain and increase only, but be content with whatever perishable things we have. If we follow Christ only for money, or to be rich and famous, we will surely fall into temptation and a snare (1 Tim. 6:6-12), into many hurtful lusts that will overflow us as flood waters, and we shall drown in destruction, condemnation, and perdition. *"For the love of money is the root of all evil which some coveted after, they have erred from the faith and pierced themselves through with many sorrows. But thou, O man of God, flee these things and <u>follow</u> after righteousness, godliness, faith, love, patience and meekness. Fight the good fight of faith; lay hold on eternal* *life"* (1 Tim. 6:10-12 and 2 Tim. 2:21-22).

The Apostle John also gives us these instructions: *"Beloved, follow not that which is evil, but that which is good. He that does is of God, but he that does evil has not seen God"* (3 Jn. 11). Contrary to some beliefs, we do not follow Christ for His great benefits or material gain, only, but the opportunity to serve Him in love, to please Him by doing His will and work while it is yet day. *"If any man serve me, let him follow me; and where I am, there shall also my servant be; if any man serve me, him will my Father honor"* (Jn. 12:26). If a blind man can follow Christ, why can't we? (Matt. 9:27) If a woman sick with an issue of blood can come to Yeshua in faith and follow, surely we can too (Matt. 9:20-22). *"For the Lord will not cast off His people, neither will He forsake His inheritance"* (Ps. 94:14-15.

It is evident that Christ loves for His sheep to follow Him. In the three-and-a-half years that His disciples did follow Him, none was cast aside, even Judas Iscariot. The Lord our Shepherd knows when one of His sheep cease to follow Him. It is virtually impossible to follow Christ if we neglect to take up our cross of love, faith, good works, the blood of Jesus and the Word of God. We have these instructions: *"Follow peace with all men, and holiness, without which no man shall see the Lord; looking diligently lest any man fail of the grace of God, lest any root of bitterness springing up to trouble you and many be defiled"* (Heb. 12:14-15). *"Come, let us return unto the Lord, for He has torn and He will heal us. He hath smitten and He will blind us up. After two days He will revive, on the third day He will raise us up and we shall live in His sight. Then we shall know, if we <u>follow on</u> to know the Lord; His going forth is prepared as the morning; and He shall come unto us as the rain, as the latter and former rain unto the Earth"* (Hos. 6:1-3). In the Old Testament covenant, Jehovah Tsidkenu did reveal Himself to His people. But today, in these latter days, as cross-bearers we are raised with Christ; He dwells within our pure hearts. We are cross-powered, having the power to reveal Jesus Christ to our enemies, power to love and to help those who hate us, and give food and drink to those who despitefully use us. As we take up our crosses to follow Christ, He Himself will flow out of our hearts as a spiritual river of life and living waters. The closer we follow Him, the more revelation of our crosses, knowledge of our hearts and of Him we will receive. While we know upon the Cross of Jesus Christ <u>He did</u> great and wonderful things for all mankind, yet *our crosses* consist of who <u>He is</u> and all that we need for Him to be, that we may be saved, holy, godly like unto Him, walking in His image and likeness, forever blessed.

Bearing Our Cross to the Crossover

"Verily, verily, I say unto you, he that heareth my word, and believeth on him that sent me, hath everlasting life, and shall not come into judgment, but is passed from death unto life" (Jn. 5:24). (See also Jn. 8:51, 1 Jn. 3:14, and Eph. 2:5)

This passing from death unto life is also a crossing over from one state of existence and consciousness unto another; from one type of life (lifestyle) unto another, and from serving the god of this world (Satan) to serve the true and living God, the Lord Jesus Christ. The words crossover and pass over are often interchangeable and relative to one another. **Webster's Dictionary** defines Crossover to mean a time or place of crossing from one side to another, to transverse, to go over; and Pass over means to proceed, travel, flow, progress as to move onward, to go on. In the above scripture, Christ, our Passover Lamb (the only way of our crossing over) revealed that our crossing over and passing over is by our believing, faith, trusting, hearing, and obeying His Word. By His cross we pass over (cross over) from death to life and by our cross we cross over from finite flesh (humanity) unto infinite spirit (godliness). Contrary to many doctrinal teachings, our crossing over is not after we exit this life, but now is the time, season, and day we must be ready and seated in our crossover position. We take up our cross to cross over from being ungodly to godly children of God, unto immortal new creatures in Christ. As we "go forth" carrying our crosses, we are changed (Job 14:14 and 2 Cor. 3:18), we are transformed (Rom. 12:2), and translated (Col. 1:13) from the inside out. God's great crossover system represents our separation from this world by the Lord's great salvation and deliverance from sin on Calvary. We have been transformed (changed, translated) from Satan's rulership to God's Kingdom. We have our cross to prove this. Just as tender and tearful as we are about the Cross of Jesus Christ, the Lord is tender and tearful about our cross and those who perish for the lack of knowledge of how to take up their crosses and cross over from finite to infinite, from man's religion to God's righteousness, holiness, from Old Testament commandments to New Testament covenants and relationships in our transition. God looks on the heart, the place of our cross, crossing and passing over from finite flesh to infinite spirit. As we take up our crosses, something beautiful takes place deep within our spirits. We have an inner transition (shift, turn, realignment, development), a spiritual transformation (reconstruction, transfiguration, makeover) that supports our change (renewal, conversion, being switched) into an everlasting *"it is finished"* position. We know we have passed (crossed over) from death unto life, because we love the brethren. *"He that loveth not his brother abideth in death"* (1 Jn. 3:14). Yet there are some who still live by their carnal flesh, believing they are saved, holy, and righteous in their own minds (Sunday-only church folks, churchologists). These are they who have yet to pass over and are not truly biblically saved in their hearts and souls (See Matt. 7:21-23). While they have a form of godliness, they have failed to *"seek ye first the Kingdom of God"* (Matt. 6:33, 7:13, 14 and 22-23). These have yet to take up their crosses and follow Christ, and <u>escape</u> from sin, death, hell, and this world system (Ecc. 7:25-26, Heb. 2:1-4 and 2 Pet. 2:18-20). Do not misunderstand. Carrying our crosses to cross over while we yet live is mandatory. No man can carry his own cross as a woman; neither can any woman carry her cross as a man. Yet God had made a way for all to escape, an escape route that is fail-safe, which is to take up our crosses, cling to the Cross of Christ, that we may cross over and escape (avoid) worldly sins, rejection, the wrath of God, and eternal condemnation that is soon to come. Even though our cross is individual, it stands in a corporate position as the Church, the body of Christ.

Because we have switched from Satan to God, and from death to life, we have a new address in destiny, a new relocation and residence, called "*The Heart of God,*" and have been made the righteousness of God in Christ (2 Cor. 15:21 and Rom. 5:19). We were dead in our sins, but are now made alive unto God as the people of God's presence, His body and earthly temple. Let us not forget that we were crucified with Christ (Gal. 2:20 and 5:24), we were buried with Him (Rom. 6:4 and Col. 2:12), we were risen with Him (Col. 2:12 and 3:1), and through salvation and grace we cross over with Him through the contents of our crosses. We cross over, go over, pass over, and flow over unto holiness, righteousness, the Word of Truth, redemption, and justification.

In church leadership there is a crossing over from a believer to a disciple, from a deacon to pastor, from teacher to prophet, and from evangelist to apostle. As we carry our cross, we put on the whole armor of God, the breastplate of righteousness, the gospel of peace, the shield of faith, the helmet of salvation, and the sword of the Spirit, which is the Word of God (Eph. 6:10-18). We have cast off our old man of sin, false religious doctrines, and man's traditions. No longer do we deny the powers of love, faith, the Word, prayer, and God's presence (2 Tim. 3:5 and 2:12). (See also Tit. 1:16 and 2 Pet. 2:1) As a young believer, I was very religious. The only crossing over I knew about and believed in was after physical death. The more I began to carry my cross and manifest its contents, it was revealed that religion has no answer for sin, neither does it save or deliver anyone from death, hell, and the grave. As I searched for truth and more of God's presence in my life, I came to understand that ignorance (lack of knowledge) was my real problem. In error I believed religion was the most important thing in my life. How wrong I was! It wasn't until I began to take up my cross and cross over from <u>religion to relationship</u> and from the image of humanity to the likeness and image of God, that I learned the more important things of salvation as a Christian, such as a new heart, a sound, renewed mind, spirit baptism, a daily relationship with God, a new birth, prayer, and being a new born again creature.

While common religion is able to take us to the doors of salvation and grace, yet it had no keys or power to carry us into the throne room of God's presence that we may cross over into holiness, righteousness, and salvation unto a new creature that's sanctified, holy, and having a right relationship with Jesus Christ. This comes only when we take up our crosses and cross over! While we were being prepared to cross over with our crosses, God had already prepared Jesus to cross over before us. He stands as <u>Jesus the Word of God</u> (God the Word) (Jn. 1:1-14, 1 Jn. 5:7 and Rev. 19:13), <u>Jesus the Love of God</u> (Jn. 3:16, 15:9-13, and 1 Jn. 4:7-21), <u>Jesus the Faith of God</u> (Mk. 11:20, Eph. 3:17 and Heb. 12:1-2) *[Note: this faith (pistis) includes our belief, trust, hope, and assurance]*, <u>Jesus Christ our blood donor</u> (Matt. 26:28, Eph. 1:7, Col. 1:20 and Rev. 1:5), the Lord of our new blood covenant, <u>Jesus our Savior and Salvation</u> (Jn. 3:17, Eph. 2:5-8, Tit. 2:10-14 and Heb. 2:3), and <u>Jesus Christ the Way, the Truth, and the Life</u> (Jn. 10:1-5 and 14:6).

Ignorantly, as a pastor I would encourage every church member to renew their church membership every year, but the real need was for them to renew their mind each and every day and to cross over in Christ. Our spirit man is well able to go places that our flesh man cannot go, even into God's very presence. Fervent prayer will surely take us there. We must become cross-wise, cross-minded, cross-connected, and cross-bearing believers, crossing over unto our divine call of God, destiny and our new covenant position. Jesus Christ is our cross and crossover, our Passover Lamb that was slain (1 Cor. 14:20 and 2 Cor. 6:16-18). As we follow Him to know and touch Him, we learn there is nothing more exciting than a *God Encounter*. Abraham had a God encounter (Gen. 12:1-7 and 17:1-17), Moses had a God encounter (Ex. 3:1-5), and King Solomon had a God encounter (1 Kgs. 3:3-15 and 11:1-9). The Apostle Paul had a God encounter on the Damascus road (Acts 26:12-19) as well as the 120 disciples on the day of Pentecost. <u>Never</u> must we enter into His presence without high expectations to encounter (coming together, meeting, to have contact with) God, to touch Him, dance with Him, cross over and be swept away. When this happens, we find ourselves outside of ourselves into deep waters far beyond humanity. We open our hearts and minds wide for Him to fill them again and again. Our hearts shall run over as a great waterfall overflowing. He is there; we are caught up in heavenly places in glory, and have crossed over from humanity to divinity, from finite to infinite, and from flesh to spirit. This crossing over is truly a marvelous thing among true worshippers in the sanctuary of God. In our history books, we have many accounts of great crossings of men over rivers, valleys, and lands by early settlers and founders, which were very important. Israel and Moses crossed over (passed over) the Red Sea on dry ground (Ex. 14:13-30), and Joshua crossed the overflowing Jordan River at flood time (Josh. 3:1-17 and 4:19-24), which was a natural miracle of God's fulfilling promise to take them unto the *Promised Land*. Yet the greater crossing is of the Spirit, wherein we take up our crosses, follow the Lord, and cross over into God's heart as sons and daughters. Here are some blessings to consider in crossing over:

- We become biblically saved (Eph. 2:5-8 and Tit. 3:5) and changed (2 Cor. 3:18 and Heb. 1:12)
- We go from defeat to victory (1 Cor. 15:57), from the unholy (1 Tim. 1:9) to holy and walk in holiness (Rom. 6:19-22)
- We transcend from an old, sinful, and carnal man to a new, saved, and holy creature in Jesus Christ (Eph. 4:22-24 and Col. 3:9-10)

- From being spiritual bastards to sons of God (Rom. 8:14-17, Heb. 12:8 and 1 Jn. 3:1-3) and from the ungodly (Ps. 1:1-7, 18:4 and 1 Tim. 1:9) to godliness (2 Pet. 1:3-7 and 2:9)
- From flesh and carnal humanity, to being born again unto a new birth in Christ (Jn. 3:3-5), unto a new creature (2 Cor. 5:17).
- From being unclean (Eze. 36:29, Rom. 1:24 and Eph. 5:5) to clean (1 Jn. 1:7-9), and sanctified in Christ (Acts 26:18, 1 Cor. 1:2 and 6:11)
- From sin and death (Jn. 5:24, 8:51 and Rom. 6:18-22), to a new life eternal (Jn. 3:14, 3:15 and 10:10), and everlasting (Lk. 18:30 and 1 Tim. 1:16)
- From finite flesh to infinite spirit (Phil. 4:13)
- From unrighteousness (Is. 55:7 and Rom. 1:18) to righteousness (2 Cor. 5:21 and Eph. 4:24) (See also Gal. 5:16-22)
- From having a sinful heart (Ps. 78:37 and Acts 8:21) to a new, pure, and right heart in Christ (Eze. 36:26 and Rom. 7:6)
- From a wicked and defiled carnal mind (Pr. 21:27, Rom. 8:7 and Tit. 1:15) unto a rightful mind (Lk. 8:35), a renewed mind (Rom. 12:2), even the mind of Christ (1 Cor. 2:16)
- From faithless (Jn. 20:27) to faith (Mk. 11:22 and Heb. 10:38), unto being the faithful in Christ (Nehemiah 9:8, Eph. 1:1 and Rev. 17:14)
- From our old man of sin (Eph. 4:22-24) unto a new man in Christ (Col. 3:9-11), having our names written in the Lamb's Book of Life (Rev. 20:12-15)
- From enemies of the cross (Phil. 3:18), God haters (Rom. 1:30), to God lovers (Matt. 22:37 and Thess. 3:5) and friends
- From children of darkness (Jn. 3:19 and Acts 26:17-18), having a dark, evil heart (Rom. 1:21 and Eph. 4:17) to children of light (Jn. 8:12, Eph. 5:8 and 1 Pet. 2:9). Let us be mindful of the fact that Satan (Lucifer, Beelzebub, the devil, Mephistopheles) is a double-cross, a double-crossing spirit; he is a two-timer, a deceiver, one who abandons and rules in false religions, sin, and death, even the crossdressing of a gay lifestyle.

All who have crossed over in Christ no longer seek for a Promised Land, but are enjoying a promising position with the Lord *our promise keeper.* None are bound by spiritual ignorance and poverty, but are full of the riches of wisdom, faith, knowledge, love, and understanding. No longer are we under Satan's power and crosses, but God's favor, grace, and crosses as children of the Kingdom of God. We cry unto the Lord, saying: *"Lord, hide your ears from the words of my mouth, and your eyes from all my sins, the unholy and ungodly thoughts and imaginations of my heart."* No longer are the plagues of worldly, wicked thoughts and imaginations prevailing in our lives, but we are washed clean, pure, and made holy by spiritual water, blood, the works of faith and the Word of the Lord. We have entered into His eternal glory, which may be defined as **The Final Frontier.** *"At that day ye shall know that I am in my Father and ye in me, and I in you"* (Jn. 14:20). (See also Jer. 3:14)

Though we may cross over, pass over, and experience the Lord, we must become divinely connected for our final frontier (perimeter, limits, boundary line) and episodes of spiritual life. While our cross and crossover give us a right position, our being connected gives us our heritage (inheritance) as son and daughters in Christ. In the Old Testament covenant, the final frontier was God with us, but in the New Testament covenant, it is God in us, working with and through us. **Webster's Dictionary** defines the word *connected* to mean joined together, united, coupled, tied or knitted together. Various dictionaries also define the word *connection* to mean relationship, kinship, association, and to be attached and bonded together, as in a marriage. We are hooked to the word of God, inseparable from His love, empowered by His Spirit, and infused into the body of Christ. In the great intercessory prayer unto His Father (Jn. 17:21-23), we can see the Lord's burning desire and will to be connected with His disciples forever in oneness and love.

"That they all may be one, as thou, Father, art in me, and I in thee, that they also may be one in us; that the world may believe that thou hast sent me. And the glory which thou gavest me I have given them, that they may be one even as we are one: I in them, and thou in me, that they may be made perfect in one; and that the world may know that thou hast sent me, and hast loved them as thou hast loved me."

We must conclude that our crossing over (passing over) takes us unto another level in Christ unto a deeper flowing of a relationship and a higher flowing of love waters being divinely connected to godliness in the highest spiritual position, which is in His love likeness and image. From the moment of true repentance, we make a spiritual connection with the Lord and begin to grow in knowledge, in truth, unto more godliness, love likeness and image of God. Our cross makes this possible through the Cross of Jesus Christ. In the process of time, we become like Christ, flowing forth with Him as a river of life and living waters unto this world system. We have His mind, we are His body, and we are God-filled new creatures <u>in</u> Christ, walking in His likeness and power. This is the final frontier!

While religion may give our souls a divine emotional encounter, it is only through righteousness, faith, change and cross bearing that we become connected to God's final frontier. Jesus Christ, the Lamb of God, was disconnected from God on Calvary for our connection with Him in glory (Is. 53:8 and Mk. 15:34). Being connected to His cross by our cross in a born again position as a new creature in Christ, and having crossed over, we can be assured that our inner rivers of His blood, love, word, and living waters shall never cease to flow. We are bound for God's eternal and final frontier. For our comfort as we go forth, the Lord continually disconnects our enemies and all evil from us (Deut. 7:15-18). The more we increase our faith (through obedience), the more firmly we become divinely connected to El Shaddai the Lord Jesus Christ, the God of our final frontier! *It's a matter of the Heart of the Cross.*

Chapter 6:
Contrasting The Cross Of Jesus Christ And Our Cross

Webster's Dictionary defines the word contrast or contrasting to mean to point out the differences between one another, to show differences when compared by contrast, and point them out. As I seek to construe (explain, define, decipher) both crosses, my passion and purpose is to inspire every believer to *take up their cross and follow Jesus Christ daily*! By contrasting our cross and the Cross of Jesus Christ, I believe the Lord will impart unto the church body knowledge, education, revelation of our cross and the Cross of Jesus Christ with clear understanding and in-depth information.

In Psalm 17:15, I was inspired to contrast David in the likeness of the Lord: "*As for me, I will be satisfied when I awake with thy likeness.*" He was a shepherd over God's sheep, a protector of Israel. He fought for Israel and was their king. The Apostle John wrote in 1 John 3:2, saying: "*Beloved now are we the children of God, and it does not yet appear what we shall be, but we know that, when He shall appear we shall be like Him; for we shall see Him as He is.*" (See also 4:17) In contrasting, we are sons of God like unto Jesus. We carry Him in our hearts as God did. We do the works of Jesus, and walk by faith, just as He did. The Lord Himself was created in our likeness (Heb. 2:17), as we are in His. (See Phil. 2:7-8 and 3:20-21) As I began to focus and contrast my own cross that I am commanded to bear with the Cross of Christ, I realized the Lord died in vain for those who refuse to take up their crosses and follow Him. We know there is none like Him and all that He did, He did for us, in us, and through us. Yet we are heirs of God, joint heirs with Jesus Christ, sons and daughters, God's earthly inheritance, holy because He is holy, and we are righteous because He is righteous. So often we look at a picture, but we do not get the picture's meaning and all that it is saying in truth. Our natural eyes may be open while our spiritual eyes are closed. We often see not, hear not, speak not, or do not; that causes us not to be able to contrast properly. Yet by grace we are the body of Christ, His holy temple, children of God, and crucified with Christ. This too is a matter of the heart and its contents. I believe God has given me grace and mercy to contrast both crosses to stir up the zeal of His people that they may take up their crosses daily and be His disciples. On Calvary, Jesus Christ died for us, but upon our cross we die daily for Him (1 Cor. 15:31). In contrasting, we are firmly positioned in a winners' circle because upon the Cross of Christ we receive forgiveness of sins, His great salvation both natural and spiritual provision, power, purpose, life eternal; and yet upon our crosses we have a relationship with God, fellowship, the love of God, His presence, riches, faith, and the living Word of God. God's representatives. The Cross of Christ was a one-time event of God, while our crosses are a daily and mandatory way of life until we die. Just as the Cross of Christ was His free choice, our cross is our free choice to choose Jesus Christ as our personal Lord and Savior.

In every case the heart is the key power and place of contrasting, for He has given us a new heart like unto His very own. The heart of our cross is the best spiritual GPS system (guide and instructor) on this planet to lead and guide us in the way of truth to heavenly places in Christ, unto His likeness and image. The Cross of Christ both naturally and spiritually came into being by the evil hands and works of ungodly men, but our cross by a holy, merciful, loving, and forgiving God. By our obedience in carrying our crosses, we validate, magnify, and authenticate the Cross of Jesus Christ in our lives. Our cross is visible and operable by the contents of His cross at work in us. We must continually study (2 Tim. 2:15) the Cross of Jesus Christ that we may come to know our very own cross to bear. As we carry our crosses, we stay focused and firmly connected to the Cross of Christ as an unbreakable union, bond, and in oneness of heart for God's approval. In Luke 10:18-21, Jesus rejoiced (celebrated, became overjoyed, took pleasure in, and was delighted). I believe He looked beyond His cross unto our crosses and saw their glory, great benefit, and eternal value as His dwelling place. The more we put our faith in the Cross of Christ, the more of our crosses we shall see, and walk in victory over this world, sin, our flesh, and the devil. Let me be very clear. I am not speaking of our flesh man, but our spirit man, called our "New Creature" in Christ, that is born again and biblically saved.

By bearing our crosses, we become authentic sons and heirs of God (Rom. 8:14-17), the Lord's bride (Is. 61:10 and Jn. 3:29), and the body of Christ (1 Cor. 6:15 and Eph. 5:30). Daily we become (are made) more in God's likeness and image (Gen. 1:26 and 1 Jn. 3:2), His dwelling place (2 Cor. 6:16-18), having more of the mind of Christ (1 Cor. 2:16). Christ was made sin for us by His cross and we are made righteousness and holiness unto Him by our crosses. Just as He was obedient to His cross, we have the power (strength) of obedience unto God through our crosses. The Cross of Christ was seen openly unto the whole wide world, our cross is made personal, individual, as in secret according to our faith and call of God. At the Cross of Christ we see light (truth, understanding, word), for He is the light, and as we take up our cross <u>we become</u> light (enlighten, visible, as a lamp) and others see Him in us. The two thieves had their own crosses to bear, Christ had His own cross, and we have ours. There are no sins, iniquities, sickness, disease, poverty, shame, or heavy burdens upon our crosses. As commonly believed, they were all nailed to the Cross of Jesus Christ. We overcome them daily by the word of God, escape from them through faith, and are kept free by the blood of the crucified Lamb of God. The more we *take up our cross*, the less sin and unrighteousness has the power to take us up. Just as Christ defeated the devil on His cross, the devil remains defeated upon our crosses. Today Christ is seated upon our crosses in a resurrected position, governing the articles of our spiritual hearts, such as faith, love, His blood and Word so that we should be saved and never die (Jn. 11:25-26). Upon His cross, Christ became something that He was not, but upon our crosses He becomes all we need Him to be. We do not carry our crosses by our own power and might, but also by the Holy Spirit, our helper who lives within us. While the Cross of Christ was naturally built of dead wood and lifeless nails, our crosses are spiritually made of love alive, the spirit of life, faith, and the living Word of God. Though Christ carried His cross for one day, we carry our crosses by faith and love all the days of our lives. The natural blood and water of Jesus Christ at some point did cease upon His cross, but flows spiritually out of our hearts and crosses as a fountain of living waters without ceasing.

It must be noted that God the Father (and Christ's disciples) forsook the Cross of Christ (Mk. 14:50), yet God will never forsake our cross. As the disciples of Christ, we too must never forsake our crosses, regardless of life's troubles, trials, and woes that will surely come. Our crosses determine our relationship approval and connection with God, but the Cross of Christ determined God's relationship and connection with sinful man. We touch God and come to know Jesus Christ through the crossways of spiritual life. He touches us and we come to know who He is, who we are and need to be. While I am very critical of my own authorship, I tremble at the responsibility of writing about the oneness connection of our cross and the awesomeness and expository values of the Cross of Jesus Christ. Christ suffered the guilt and shame of His cross that we may be found innocent, guiltless, no longer sinners, criminals, and enemies of God. Just as He was left alone to die a lonely, painful, and sinful death, all who take up their crosses come alive to enjoy a glorious, victorious, rich, and wonderful life. Yet there are constraining issues. Modern religion has sought to instruct both new and old believers to "kneel and bow down at the foot of the Cross of Christ," and have grossly neglected to instruct them how to bow down upon their own crosses where Jesus Christ now lives.

The more we give honor and glory unto Calvary, the more we come to know our own crosses, their purpose, importance, and power. Jesus Christ was our suffering Savior upon His cross, but upon our crosses He rules victorious as Lord of Lords and King of Kings. He is the fullness and substance of our crosses that are alive, eternal, blessed and God-approved. From our crosses He speaks to all who come into our presence, saying: *"Look upon Me. I love you. Can you see Me? You may touch Me. Come receive Me, take hold of Me, carry Me and you will be saved."* Let me say again that the Cross of Christ was birthed as the result of man's evil works, wicked minds and hearts; but our cross is birthed from the loving hands of God, our faith in God, obedience, salvation, His works of righteousness, holiness and truth. Most certainly it's a matter of man's ideology and theology that rules over the more important articles called "knee-ology." The natural Cross of Christ was an outer cross seen and ruled by man, but our crosses are inner crosses that are seen and ruled by God.

Jesus Christ today lives within us by the contents of our crosses that determine our spiritual life, destiny, the state of our minds, and the condition of our hearts. Yet I believe every lost sinner who would be saved must look to the Cross of Christ first, but after salvation and being born again they must take up their own crosses and follow the Lord, steadfastly looking unto Jesus, the heart of their crosses, the author and finisher of their faith. Satan hates our crosses. This is because believers are alive and well, having all dunamis power over him and all of his ungodly works and crosses. He knows that by our crosses, he is defeated, and by the Cross of Christ, he is eternally condemned. At Easter time each year, as the lost world looks upon the Cross of Christ, we must also show them our crosses and the joy of life that awaits them if they repent and come to Jesus Christ and bear their crosses, freely given by a changed heart, a new and right mind. It may be said like this: on the old rugged cross at Calvary hung the heart of God and a new cross for every believer. Our cross was also finished the moment the Roman soldier pierced the Lord in His side (heart) and out flowed His precious blood and water. Our salvation, new birth, and divine relationship are predicated upon the Lord's cross factors of spiritual life. The saying of old is now made clear: If there is no cross, there can be no crown. Just as Jesus Christ is the fullness of the Godhead Trinity (Col. 2:9), He is also the fullness of our crosses, their contents and power. <u>He is love</u> (1 Jn. 4:16), <u>the Word</u> (Jn. 1:1-4), <u>our righteousness</u> (2 Pet. 1:1), <u>our peace</u> (Eph. 2:14), joy (Jn. 15:11), <u>the truth</u> (Jn. 14:16), <u>our salvation</u> (2 Tim. 2:10), and the Word of life, to name a few. Therefore, by contrasting we can conclude that our spiritual cross is the fullness of Jesus Christ within our hearts (Jn. 1:16, Eph. 3:19 and 4:13). There is always good news flowing from the Cross of Jesus Christ and there is also good news flowing out of our cross, where He now lives.

We can believe and confess that Christ died upon His cross for us that we might have life upon our crosses for Him! The more we carry our cross, we die to self, sin, Satan, and this world system. My heart's prayer is this: *"Lord, give me a clean mouth to speak Your word, a renewed mind to do Your will, an anchored soul that I may carry my cross and not stumble, fall, or experience spiritual heart failure."*

Though we show our faith through the Cross of Christ, we live by faith through the flowing blood, word and water out of our crosses. By carrying our crosses daily, we do not deny, abolish, or delete the Cross of Christ, but we magnify it, enhance it, and establish our crosses deeper into our lives, having a greater understanding and a right and better relationship with God. When we ignorantly refuse to take up our crosses and follow Christ, we are also ignorantly standing against the Cross of Christ, and this is not acceptable. I say again that none can bear their cross without being born again, biblically saved, and walking in the Kingdom of God. Our crosses are the way of God's Kingdom within our hearts, having Jesus Christ there as our Lord and King. Cross bearing is a sure sign of our being children of God, sons, daughters, heirs, and the true body of Christ. In truth, our crosses are an extension of the cross at

Calvary. The Lord is its creator, owner, keeper, and provider. Being made by Him alone, our crosses belong to Him and He freely gives a personal cross unto all who will faithfully follow Him. The old wooden cross at Calvary belonged to those who did build it. The more we take up our crosses, the spiritual Cross of Christ increases in its power, purpose, value, and importance in our Christian walk of life. Before Christ hung suspended between Heaven and hell, man's destiny was predicated upon a <u>finite</u> foundation ruled by his obedience to laws, ordinances, and commandments that very few did obey. Christ came forth in full obedience. He died and rose from the grave on the third day and entered into mankind at Pentecost. All who received Him into their hearts could now stand upon an <u>infinite</u> foundation of grace through faith, having a new birth, a new love, heart, life, and blood covenant. The Cross of Christ is magnified to its maximum when coupled with our crosses with understanding. By revelation we can see how both crosses now stand locked together and infused forever in an inseparable oneness position.

While it would take a lifetime to contrast the *Heart of the Cross* of Christ and our crosses, yet we can rest in the fact that we are drawn closer to the Lord by the contents of His cross and He is drawn closer to us by the contents of our crosses. We must remember our body is His Holy Temple today and our crosses within our hearts are His most Holy Place, where the Lord sits and rules as *Three of One Kind*. This cannot be denied. In the doctrine of oneness in deity, He is one God in three, but in the doctrine of the Trinity in deity He is three persons (Gods) in one Godhead that works as God the Father in creation, God the Son in redemption, and God the Holy Spirit in the end time church. These too are one. Even though these three are one eternal Spirit at work, the doctrines of men, man's theology, traditions, and religions separate into hundreds of different beliefs through the spirit of separatism, and division. Jesus gave us the answer, saying: "Hear O Israel: the Lord our God is one Lord." (Mk. 12:29) (See Zech. 14:9, Eph. 4:4-6 and 1 Tim 2:5, 6, 16) In John 10:30, "I and my Father are one." (Is. 9:6 and Jn. 14:6-11) No heart can bear three gods.

While many see the Trinity in different categories and perspectives, the <u>Gospel of the Heart of the Cross</u> gives honor and truth to at least four more attributes of God, such as *"God the Word"* (Jn. 1:1-14, 1 Jn. 5:7-8 and Rev. 19:13), *"God the Lord"* (Ps. 100:3, Matt. 4:7 and Rev. 19:1), *"God the Redeemer"* (Ps. 78:35, Is. 63:16, Eph. 1:7), and "*God the Savior*" (Ps. 106:21, Is. 43:3, 1 Tim. 1:1, 4:10 and Tit. 1:3-4). Yet in the Cross of the Heart, it is "*God the Word*" who reveals all things, especially of the Cross of Jesus Christ. Without "*God the Word*" and Jesus Christ the perfect Word made flesh (the Lord of Perfection), all godliness that can be known is no less than vanity. This is because all that God has to give comes unto us in a perfect love, perfect word state, in a finished position for our perfect hearts, where therein lies perfect faith, God's perfect love, will, peace, salvation, and word, that we may walk in perfect heavenly places, His Most Holy Place. As we view the Most Holy Place called our heart or the Heart of God, we come to know the Spirit of Christ (Rom. 8:9 and Gal. 4:6), the Holy Spirit (Gen. 1:1-2, Rom. 5:5 and 1 Jn. 5:7), and the Spirit of God (Matt. 3:16, Jn. 4:23 and Rom. 8:14) that are all one Spirit at work in three seasons and dispensations for our salvation, redemption, and life's great benefits. We call these three <u>God in us</u>; one God, one Spirit, and one heart. The oneness of the Trinity is infinite and can only be correctly discerned by infinite and godly believers, who know that God the Son only does and speaks what God the Father does and says, and God the Holy Spirit only does and speaks whatever God the Son says and does. Therefore, Jesus Christ upon His cross and our cross is all of God that anyone will ever need. In Ephesians 4:4-6, there is only one body and one Spirit, one hope of our calling; one Lord, one faith, <u>one God</u> and Father of all who is above all, through all and <u>in</u> you all. (Tit. 2:10-13, and Is. 45:18-23) No one can be godly without God, saved without the Savior, or redeemed without the Redeemer. Our cross is never unclean because of the indwelling presence of God's cleansing faith (Acts 15:9), His cleansing word (Jn. 15:3), and the cleansing blood of Jesus Christ (Rev. 1:5). I say again that the Most Holy Place within us is not made by the hands of men, but by the hands of God. Only God can make us a new heart, a perfect heart, and a new, perfect creature. Imperfection is not acceptable upon our crosses.

Just as God Eloheim Himself is never greater than His very own heart, we are never greater than our very own hearts. All of the great blessing and great things that have been done, are being done, or are planned to do from our cross and the Cross of Jesus Christ will be done from His heart with all of His heart, even His Most Holy Place, for He is the *Most High God*, the *Holy One* of Israel (Ps. 21:7, 78:56, Is. 12:6, Daniel 3:26, Acts 1:48 and Heb. 7:1). Just as He has entered into our hearts, we must enter into His heart as well, and become cross-bearing and cross-connected.

Our revivals, conferences, and church services must now be filled with spiritual crosses and hearts that contain Agape love, God's word, faith, blood of the Cross, and life-waters of salvation for a greater manifestation and demonstration of the presence of the Lord Jesus Christ. Church leaders must cease seeing only bodies that fill their sanctuary and without seeing the personal cross each church member carries within their perfect hearts. They must cease to view only the bodies of the people, but view their hearts, where Jesus lives. Every sermon they preach and every message they teach must be for and from the heart, which is the place and power of every cross. As we lift up our hands and hearts to enter into deep waters of prayer, praise and worship, we lift up our spiritual crosses with our pure hearts and clean hands unto God.

Just as God called His only begotten Son to His cross, He is calling all His people to their cross that they may live, become cross-connected, cross-bearing, cross-created in Christ, and fully prepared to cross over into eternal life. Man physically took Christ to His cross, but the Holy Spirit spiritually takes us to our crosses. Whether to sinner or saint, heathen or believer, the Lord's arms are stretched out still and He speaks unto all mankind worldwide, saying: "*Come, take up your cross and follow Me!*"

Just as love was/is the power of the Cross of Christ, it is also the power of our crosses. Carrying our crosses gives us the authority to have a continual intimate love affair with the Lord as His bride and body. This too is another reason we must take up our crosses daily and follow Him.

Though all His disciples left Him to bear His cross alone, none of them would forsake their own crosses after His resurrection on the third day. Let me say again, our crosses are perfect; there is no imperfection, all of their contents demand perfect hearts in which to dwell (1 Kgs. 8:61, 15:14 and Matt. 5:48). While the death of Jesus Christ on Calvary was so great and priceless, we must never forget the importance of His rising on the third day as He had promised (Acts 10:39-40). By His rising, our crosses became sure, firmly established, unmovable, priceless, eternal, and full of glory. We come to know Him there, His love, word, faith, presence, His deep wells of salvation and Holy Spirit, all mandatory for our daily walk with the Lord. Without the Holy Spirit it is impossible for us to take up our crosses and follow Him in the church services, revivals, rivers, and living concepts of spiritual life. Yet the Lord is faithful, loving, kind, forever moving, and He is pouring out His Holy Spirit upon all flesh. Our cross gives us carte blanche access to His grace, all He is, and all we need Him to be.

When Satan or our enemies look upon us to war, steal, kill, and destroy, and they behold our cross, the blood and water flowing forth as living water, they will surely flee from us. From the day of repentance and salvation, we became heirs of our cross, even joint heirs of the Cross of Jesus Christ that gives us power, grace, and the right to walk in God's presence, walking in His perfect will, love, word, faith, and to become more like Him in His likeness and image. This pleases the Lord our Shepherd when He sees His people following Him, carrying their crosses. He sees more of Himself. God loves to see His own likeness and image in the Earth. He loves to behold Himself in us, and His glory cloud does follow us. Leaders are commanded to "feed God's sheep." Proper spiritual feeding and nutrition help the people of God to have the strength to carry their crosses. Should they become hungry or thirsty, they may spiritually drink of the water and blood of the cross, even to eat of the body of Christ (Jn. 4:13-14 and 6:54-55).

Recently, I went to a water purification presentation, a seminar held by a local church. All were giving praise and glory to a new water machine that could take defiled, unclean tap water and make it 99.99 percent pure. This great machine cost $3,900; many were excited and willing to pay the price. As they drank the purified water that was once defiled, I began to tell them about the greater importance of inner purity of our heart, mind, body, soul, and spirit. We must have the cleansing power and the watering power of God's Word, faith, and blood that purifies and is freely given by God through His cross unto us. While pure food and drink are very important, there is nothing better than a pure heart and a clean mind that give us the strength to carry our crosses.

Christ upon His cross was the despised and rejected Son (the denied son), but upon our crosses, He is the acceptable Lord of Lords, King of Kings, El Shaddai, our Savior, and God the Word. He is the fullness of our crosses the same as He is the fullness of the Godhead bodily (Col. 2:9). God wants fullness and we become fullness in Christ (Eph. 3:19). We ask God to keep us full of our crosses. Our crosses demand a heart full of God. Godly fullness determines our relationship, connection, association, bonding, friendship, and fellowship with God (1 Cor. 1:9 and 1 Jn. 1:36). As cross bearers, we are the light of the world and His word is a lamp unto our feet. No one ever needs a lamp or light unless they are going somewhere. We are on the move for Jesus Christ. We have a destiny and a destination as we run this Christian race. Where there is no cross, there is no source of power or energy that we may be able to walk or run with the Lord. Both crosses are our energy source and our power of Christian love. Because of God's great cross within us, we are expected to do greater works than Jesus did (Jn. 14:12). Our cross bearing is a sure sign and assurance that all our sins are forgiven, and our names have been written in the Lamb's Book of Life.

By the death of His cross, the Lord received the power and authority to be the God of our crosses and hearts, which are His earthly dwelling place. He has spoken saying: "*I will dwell <u>in them</u> and walk in them; and I will be their God and they shall be my people*" (2 Cor. 6:16). (See also Eze. 37:26-27) From within, He wants to guard our hearts, guide our footsteps, and connect our crosses to His cross through spiritual life. He knows we cannot make it through life on our own, being disconnected. As we bear our holy cross of God, we can be sure that our faith wells, love rivers, Word and blood fountains shall never run dry.

I say this unto every lost sinner that they contrast their cross of Satan with the Cross of Jesus Christ and choose life, remembering that by the Cross of Christ all sin, condemnation, and eternal death have been eradicated and exterminated, and a new cross of salvation, freedom, and life is made available free of charge.

Summary Viewpoints of Our Cross and the Cross of Jesus Christ, For Information, Learning, Education, Revelation, and Demonstration

- The Cross of Jesus Christ was created and set in place by sin, death, and the evil works of the hands of wicked men. While our cross is set in place by God's love, grace, faith, salvation, the blood and water of the cross by the will and hands of God.
- The Cross of Christ now stands in an "*it is finished*" position, but our cross is a new beginning every day. As followers of God, we take it up by faith daily in a never-ending infinite position and eternal love relationship.
- While on the Cross at Calvary Christ became sin for us, upon

- our crosses He is Lord, our living Savior, risen King, and we are His temple, righteousness and body, the Church.
- Acts 15:18, says God knows (and knew) all His works from the beginning of this world. As wicked men were building a cross for Jesus Christ, our crosses were already made and completed in Him (Christ).
- Because our crosses are a spiritual manifestation of the Cross of Christ, they cannot (or will not) function without His presence and finished work on Calvary.
- While Jesus suffered and died <u>on</u> His cross by the hands of men, He now lives <u>in</u> our heart, alive upon our crosses by the hands and power of God. He is alive forever more.
- While the contents of the Cross of Christ were sin, death, sickness and disease, separation from God, iniquity, and anti-God principles, the contents of our crosses are love, salvation, faith, joy, peace, the blood of the Lamb of God, God's Word and grace (to name a few).
- At the Cross of Jesus Christ, Satan and his demons and devils rejoiced even for a few days, but at our cross the Lord Himself rejoices, and Satan is defeated.
- The Cross of Christ was finite (limited, restricted, measurable), our crosses in Christ are infinite (unlimited, endless, boundless, eternal). On Calvary He died as finite, but upon our crosses He lives and rules infinite, forever.
- The Cross of Christ stood for crucifixion, suffering, death, burial, and resurrection; our crosses stand for love, grace, God's Word, salvation, and life eternal.
- The manmade natural crosses stood high on the hill at Calvary, leading all to death, but our invisible spiritual crosses lie deep within us, made by the hands of God, leading all to blessings, spiritual prosperity, and life eternal.
- While sin, death, and hell were the primary issues of the Cross of Christ, love, life, and relationship are the great issues of our crosses.
- Upon the Cross of Christ, sin and death ruled, but our crosses are ruled by joy, life, and peace. The Cross of Christ was visible for a day, but our crosses are visible forever.
- Because Christ was victorious upon His cross, we are victorious upon our crosses.

- The sad part of the Christian life is this: the Cross of Jesus Christ can be seen upon the walls of almost every church, upon a chain or bracelet, but our crosses cannot yet be found anywhere. Our crosses in truth and fullness are Christ alive in the midst of our hearts.
- The Cross of Christ is to be *believed* as we live by our crosses through faith. Yet it is by the Cross of Jesus Christ we have the power to take up our crosses and follow Him. He took up His cross outwardly, but we take our crosses up inwardly.
- Mankind did behold, view, and observe the Cross of Christ, yet today few have beheld (or observed) their own crosses.
- The Cross of Jesus Christ is the way (only way) to salvation and eternal life and *"our cross"* is the strength of it. Upon His cross the Lord *gave His life*, while upon our crosses *He is the life*. Jesus said this: *"I am the way, the truth and the life; no man comes unto the Father, by but me"* (Jn. 14:6).
- The Cross of Christ stood in a seventy-two-hour position (three days and three nights), but now our crosses (the crosses of our hearts) are endless, timeless, and now stand forever and ever.

All things were finished in Christ from the foundations of this world. Yahweh had already built and finished a spiritual cross for every believer and was waiting for man to build a natural (physical) cross for Christ so all things might come to pass and be fulfilled. Our crosses are most loved crosses unto God. He still rejoices when He looks at the crosses of our spiritual hearts, and sees His Son and our likeness of Him. From the moment we take up our crosses, we do not remain still. We are well able to use the contents and go forth in victory and follow after Jesus Christ. This is well possible because in our heart and spirit we are well able to travel at the speed of thought. The travesty of our time is when a church is full of people who are yet empty (void) of their crosses and the knowledge of the Heart of the Cross of Jesus Christ. Our cross bearing and following gives us the right to receive showers of blessings, spiritual rivers, waters, and riches of great proportions and benefits. For all those who shall be saved by the Cross of Jesus Christ, the Lord had given one of the most important commandments of instruction found in the Bible.

Deny yourself! *Take up your cross and follow me.*

Chapter 7
Author's Journey To
The Heart Of The Cross

Author's Heart Biography:
I was born and raised in a small town in Lenapah, OK, in a family of thirteen boys and two girls. There was never enough food or clothing to go around, but somehow we managed to survive. It would take a whole book to write about the history, stories, miracles, and events of the Downing family that took place from the time of my birth until I was fully grown and married.

This brief synopsis relates how I came to know God, the Gospel of the Heart, and *The Heart of the Cross* message and heart ministry. One day, when I was twelve years old, my mother <u>pointed her hand</u> at me, and with a firm voice said: "Don, you are the preacher of the family." I thought to myself there were ten other brothers (two had died young), let one of them preach.

At the age of sixteen, I began playing in a local rock & roll band with the desire to become a star. Once again, my mother came to me and <u>pointed her hand</u> at me, saying: "Son, I see the way you are going, do not stay out there too long, for God has chosen you to preach His word." At that time, I did not have ears to hear or a heart to obey her words. To end the conversation, I promised her I would. Later in life, her hand and voice would save my life. At the age of eighteen, I was well known as a singer/musician and got married to Mary Alice Barber from Sedan, KS. In our fifth year of marriage, she was shot and killed in Wichita, KS, by a local Caucasian thug who shot her as he drove by where she sat on a motorcycle. I was hurt, devastated, and no longer wanted to live my life without her. My mother also had passed away. Coming home one morning about 2am, after performing at a night club in Washington, DC, I decided to take my own life. But when I placed the gun to my head and prepared to pull the trigger, something happened that would affect my life forever. Suddenly, from the ceiling of my room came my <u>mother's hand,</u> pointing at me, and I heard her firm, prophetic voice saying once again that I was to preach God's Word. I was shocked, speechless, yet I knew it was very serious. As I laid the gun down, I promised her again that I would, only this time I was also serious. Her hand suddenly disappeared. For the next few years in the midst of drugs, rock & roll, R&B music, alcohol, and sexual promiscuity, I told everyone about *Mama's Hand*. I began to read the Gideon Bible that I found in hotels.

There came a night when my band and I performed with one of the greatest rock & roll groups in the world at that time: KC and the Sunshine Band. I was determined not to allow them to get more applause than my band, Little Willy and the Hand Jives. Before the performance, I ingested several types of illegal drugs for energy, and during the night I drank alcohol and ingested more drugs. The battle of the bands was a tie. How I made it home that night, I do not remember. Later that night as I lay asleep (passed out) on my sofa (couch), I suddenly found myself outside my body, up against the ceiling of the room, looking down at myself on the couch. It was my first out-of-body experience. In terror and fear, I cried out to God for help as loudly as I could. He allowed me to crawl downward and reenter my body. I awoke sober, trembling, and shaken, but with a mind to leave all drugs and alcohol alone.

A year later, I moved from Washington, DC, to Virginia, where I met my second wife, Nellie Culbreath. For fifteen years, we had a good, peaceful marriage, until one day her doctor told her she had cervical cancer. The doctors did all they could for her. By this time, we had given our hearts to Jesus Christ and had joined a local church. We were biblically saved. One morning around 4am, I was awakened by what seemed like a fiery hot liquid being poured upon my throat. I screamed and opened my eyes. What I saw standing over my wife was a great angel with great wings, leaning on a staff, with eyes closed as if asleep. Fear, chills, and astonishment flooded my whole body.

My voice spoke on its own, saying: "I bind you in the name of Jesus."

Immediately its face was within an inch of my face, and for some reason I could not move my body. What I saw upon its face was hate, fear, evil, and madness to the highest degree.

When I shouted, "The blood of Jesus is against you!" it disappeared in a cloud of dust. When the dust touched my hands, my whole body became cold as ice. Shaken to my bones, I jumped out of bed (my wife was still asleep) and ran throughout the house, praying and anointing each room in the name of the Lord. When morning came, I called my pastor, Bishop Ralph E. Green, and he suggested it was an angel of death. Even though the doctor had said she was doing well, my wife of eighteen years passed away two weeks later. The day after her funeral, I stood in front of my house and made a decree to God that I would serve Him, live for Him, do His will, preach, and obey His every word. I also spoke to Satan and his demonic forces, saying I would be their enemy all of my days. I was on my way to the Cross of Jesus Christ and the ministry of the gospel of the heart.

Two years later, I married a wonderful Christian woman, Lezlie Williams, and became a deacon in the church. I didn't know at that time what the Lord had in store for me. One night as we lay talking, she saw movement in her closet. When I saw the movement, I called on the name of Jesus and out of the closet came a dragon, a red serpent. As it ran under our bed, one of its back tentacles went through my wife's body, wounding her, and then the beast smashed into my closet doors and disappeared. I prayed for my wife. I could see a very small amount of blood around her naval, but she was fine. Though I was a home improvement contractor (a door installer), nothing I found would fit the opening until the day we sold the house.

We started a Love Ministry in Lorton, VA, teaching and preaching about the power, purpose, and importance of love. As time went by, we traveled to the Far East, into China, Japan, the Philippines, Bermuda, Santo-Domingo, and several states, spreading the good news about the love of God. One weekend we decided to go away together and went to Maryland's Eastern Shore to a Holiday Inn. Again, it happened. About 4am I was awakened by a cold wind blowing upon my face. I looked toward the open window and saw the form (outline) of a man. While I could see through him to the wall behind him, there were hundreds of flashing spirits all around him. He had a dim glow and outline all around his body. It was not a dream or a vision, this time it was natural and real, not just spiritual.

I spoke to him, saying: "Satan, what are you doing in my room? My Lord and Savior defeated you on Calvary over 2,000 years ago. I bind you at your heart! I command you to leave this room right now in the name of Jesus."

Immediately he fell to the floor and turned into the largest snake I had ever seen (about twenty-five feet long) and began to crawl out the open window. It was a gruesome, chilling, and awesome sight. Later, when my wife awoke, I took her over to the window and we saw two large scales and a bent window frame where Satan had made his exit from our room.

I remembered in 2 Corinthians 11:14-15, how Satan is able to transform himself into an angel of light and his ministering demonic spirits as ministers of righteousness. I sought the Lord more fervently from that point onward. I petitioned Him daily, saying: *"Lord, I have seen Satan several times, but I haven't seen You. I want to see You, Lord! I need to see Your face!"* A few weeks later, I saw in a vision a great heart that looked to be almost a city block wide and half a mile high, going forth over a city and dropping large drops of blood upon certain houses and churches. Somehow, I knew it was the Lord at work. It was an awesome sight. It seemed to me this great heart was large enough to contain enough blood for every Christian in that city. I remembered how we are covered by the blood of the Cross of Jesus Christ, and how He has washed us in His own blood (Rev. 1:5). When I came to myself, I prayed, asking God to give me a clear understanding. He spoke into my spirit and said: *"My son, My blood not only cleanses, covers, heals, protects, and saves My people, but it is also a great defense. Every family and church that received blood from My heart had a spiritual need for the presence of My spiritual blood. Those who did not receive blood were not of Me, for they knew not My heart. I have called you out of sin and darkness, and have anointed you to write, teach, and preach the Gospel of The Heart. Go forth and tell My people that love must be from the heart."* Suddenly, understanding came. All that had happened to me in my life up to this point was Satan trying to consume, turn, and change my heart.

"My heart is love's dwelling place and God's dwelling place," I said to myself out loud. It came to me that mankind daily sees the size of God's creation but not the size of His great heart that operates the blood. A blood-filled heart, a blood pump and temperature controller

I spent the next few weeks searching out heart scriptures, meanings, and power. God gave me heart revelation, information, and the Holy Spirit taught me. From prayer, faith, love, worship, and praise to God's word, salvation and life all must be from the heart and are heart-operated. I sat down with my church workers and my wife, letting them know I was changing the name of the church from Free Gospel Church of Virginia to Heart to Heart Christian Center.

By the Spirit of God I shared with them the Gospel of the Heart, how out of the heart flows the issues of life (Pr. 4:23). With the heart man believes unto righteousness (Rom. 10:10), and wisdom reveals that no one can know God until they know His heart. Yet He knows the heart of all mankind (1 Kgs. 8:39 and Acts 1:24). God looks on the heart (1 Sam. 16:7, 2 Chron. 16:9, and Jer. 17:9-10).

A dreadful thought came to me about my own heart: Was it right with God? Or was it in need of replacement? Even though I was a well-known pastor, teacher, and man of God, my heart wasn't yet right in God's sight. I knew I needed to give the Lord my whole heart. Like unto David, I needed God to create in me a clean heart. I came to realize that many thousands of believers need a new heart that's Bible-based, one that has been washed in the blood of Jesus, a faithful, loving, clean, right, praying, and faith-filled heart. And the list goes on and on. All worship, preaching, teaching, singing, and God's Word must be from the heart. The Lord showed me the heart of His servants such as Moses, Jeremiah, Abraham, David, the prophets and the apostles. How that the heart determines our tears, thoughts, imaginations, conversation, prayer, and marriage.

I would soon learn it is all about the Gospel of the Heart and *The Heart of the Cross* of Jesus Christ. In the years to come, I would learn about God's pure, perfect, and clean heart and Satan's evil, wicked, and defiled heart. I would come to know about the many types of hearts the Lord has to give unto His people, such as pure, perfect, forgiving and clean hearts, as opposed to Satan's evil, lying, deceitful and lustful hearts. I found out the type of heart we possess determines the type of life we will live, and the place of our eternal rest.

A Musical Experience

God doesn't forget our labor of love. In 2009, He did something in my life that brought me back to reality and my true purpose in life. I had been a saved church person for over twenty-four years, moving from deacon to elder to pastor to bishop in 1996, and working toward being an apostle. I received a phone call from Rodney Lay of Rodney and The Blazers, my first real professional rock & roll bandleader in my young life. We had performed together in Kansas and Oklahoma from 1958 to 1964, until I moved to Washington, DC. Rodney called to tell me that the state of Kansas was building a museum for all the music groups who had worked to supply Kansas with music, and they wanted me to come out to Kansas and perform again. We were considered to be one of the best groups and progressive because we consisted of four white and two black musicians, which gave us a wide variety of musical choices. As Rodney and I talked, my first reaction was, *No! No way!* I explained to him I was now *saved,* and I thought this was just another trick of the devil.

A few days went by and one of the employees of the governor of Kansas called, asking me to please come. They wanted me to be the first black musician to be inducted into the Kansas State Music Hall of Fame at Lawrence, KS. When I explained unto him I was a saved, born again Christian and an ordained bishop, I was surprised when they confessed to their faith in the Lord Jesus Christ. I knew several of our band members were now saved because it was the guitar player (Anthony "Pete" Williams) who had led me to Christ many years before. Playing bass was Rodney Lay (our bandleader), on drums was Robert "Bob" York, on saxophone was Bobby Scott and Gene Bonjourni, and I played the piano and organ. The governor and music organizers agreed I could do anything I wanted to do, which included preaching the Word of God.

I caught the first flight I could and went to Kansas. When I arrived, to my surprise I learned there was also a Battle of the Bands taking place to see which of the nine groups being inducted to the Music Hall of Fame was the best. Over forty-five years had gone by since our band had performed together, and we only had time for one rehearsal. Since all of us confessed Jesus Christ as our Lord and Savior, I spent some time in His presence, asking Him for help and strength, for I had not played any secular music in over twenty years. The night of the performance at K-State University was awesome. There were about 1,400 to 1,500 people in attendance, as well as several well-known performers and the governor of the state.

We were chosen to be the second group to perform. When we went on stage, Rodney asked me if I would do the first two songs. The moment I said yes, I felt the anointing power of God, the same excitement and energy I felt just before I would preach a sermon. I didn't understand it at all. I chose to do two songs that would impact the people (ooh-poo-pa-doo) and the second was a song by Ray Charles (*Georgia On My Mind*), who had just recently passed away. The first song connected the people to us and figuratively brought them on stage with us. I had never seen such dancing, leaping, and shouting in my life! When I sang *Georgia On My Mind*, by Ray Charles, there were tears and standing ovations, giving honor and respect unto him.

As other members of the band did their songs, they were also greatly received. I stopped the whole show and asked an unexpected question: Is there anybody in this building who loves the Lord Jesus Christ? Immediately there was a multitude of lifted hands, hallelujahs, and cries of, "Thank You, Jesus," and "amen." The people gave high praise and honor unto God for about fifteen minutes, and I was able to minister Jesus Christ. All the people, including the other bands loved us. After signing about twenty autographs, I excused myself, found an empty room and began to talk to God about everything. To my surprise, He answered me clearly, saying: *"My son, you have been in church for so long you have forgotten where I am working. This world is the place of My work, preparing hearts for salvation, but in My church congregation I am there preparing hearts for My presence and eternal life. Have you forgotten where I found You and brought you from?"* Immediately I realized that because of the Cross, any heart and soul can be saved anywhere, at any time, in any sinful place, whether it is a nightclub, state or local prison, brothel, drug house, or job site. It is not a manmade building that determines the time and place of God's salvation, but the giving of the heart! It is still God's will that none should perish (Jn. 3:15 and 1 Cor. 1:18). I realized musicians also must come to the Cross of Jesus Christ for a new heart and a new life. The very next day I was blessed to hear we won first place, and our picture and testimony of Jesus were in almost every newspaper in the state of Kansas. From that day until now, regardless of race, creed, religion or place, I tell all to invite Jesus Christ into their hearts to repent of their sins, and to give God all of their hearts. I remembered a heart commandment found in Proverbs 23:26, that says: *"My son, give me thine heart, and let thine eyes observe my ways."*

I would be remiss not to mention the one person who influenced me the most concerning the heart message and ministry, a great woman of God who was God's Heart messenger in her season. For about twenty-five years, I had worked as a home improvement contractor, doing sales and installations of windows and doors. I had made an appointment with a customer who was also a widow. As we sat down to talk after I gave my sales presentation, I noticed she used the Lord's name a lot in conversation. I saw this as a prime opportunity to share with her *The Gospel of The Heart*. She sat quietly and allowed me to speak to her for about twenty minutes. As I said certain things about the heart, tears flowed from her eyes. Finally, she began to speak to me about things of the heart and heart ministry that would change my life forever. With a tear-stained face, this was her testimony: *"For over twenty-five years, I taught and preached the Gospel of The Heart. Being a woman, it was very hard, because most religions did not believe in women preachers. I told all who would hear me about the importance of a new heart, a right, good, and clean heart. Now that I am old, I have been praying to God that before I die He would send a replacement person who would come forth and continue on, telling the world about God's Heart, Satan's heart, and the power of the heart, which is God's dwelling place. God has sent you. He has anointed and chosen you. You must go forth now, for many hearts are in trouble with God."* We prayed, and as I left her home, I was encouraged and had a deeper made up mind, to proclaim the Gospel of the Heart.

My first revelation of the heart message came to me unexpectedly and did lead me from a love message to my heart ministry. There came a day as I stood up from early morning prayer, the presence of the Lord literally filled the room as a great whirlwind. As I cried out unto Him for help, He spoke to me in a stern yet loving voice, saying I would not die. He asked me several questions that would change my life and ministry forever. Where does love dwell in the earth? Where do faith, His Word, peace, joy, and wisdom dwell? Where do prayer, praise, worship, and songs come forth from and where was His dwelling place upon the Earth? Falling on my knees, I cried out, "In my heart, Lord!" With His quiet, tender voice, He told me my heart was not right with Him, He was the God of Abraham, Isaac, and Jacob! Immediately there came into my spirit a vision, the body of a man only from the waist down going through a forest and knocking down everything that stood in its way. It came to a dead carcass, turned it over and the stench was unbearable, extremely rancid and beyond description. Once again, I cried out to God for help. He spoke again, saying: *"My son, this is what your heart is like in My sight."* I wanted to tell Him I was a pastor, a teacher of love, and I knew scriptures as well as anyone, but it came to me that it was not my title, the amount of knowledge or works that determined my spiritual life but my relationship with Him and the condition of my heart. For the next three days I could feel His presence as He led me through the Bible scriptures, teaching me the

Gospel of the Heart. On the third day as I arose, I literally saw Him standing higher than the rising morning sun. I begged Him not to go, but He looked at me, turned, and began to walk away, saying; "*Go, tell my people about the Gospel of the Heart. Write it in a book that their hearts may be right in My sight. I am the God of The Heart.*" Then He was gone. For the past thirty years, as God's heart messenger I have not turned from doing that.

Having now written many books on the heart, I feel this book, *The Heart of the Cross*, is the most serious one of all. The message of the heart cries out through the message of love, God's Word, and faith, saying: "*You must know the heart of God, you must serve the heart of Jesus Christ, and love Him with all of your heart!*" We must know our own hearts and learn the hearts of our leaders, mates, family members, loved ones and friends, the hearts of our enemies and even the heart of Satan himself. It is a heart life, a heart world that is heart-ruled. I thank God for Lezlie Williams Downing, my wife and pastor of Heart to Heart Christian Center, who stood by my side for twenty-three years, a great woman of God who spoke positive words as I embraced the Gospel of the Heart Ministry as God's heart messenger for *The Heart of the Cross*. I thank you, 'boo' from the top and bottom of my heart, even though you have now departed this life to be with the Lord Jesus Christ.

A few months later, the Lord did visit me again. Just like the first visitation and manifestation, Jesus Christ came to me in a vision that changed my heart, life and ministry, wherein I became God's messenger not to just teach and preach the heart message but to establish heart ministries worldwide. In His second visitation, He was much more firm and His visage was extremely more serious. As I look back, I believe He revealed Himself to me knowing that soon He would send me forth into the church having the Gospel of the Heart and knowledge of the Heart of the Cross wherein lies both life and death. I had been looking to see Him again face to face, to worship and rejoice in His presence, giving Him thanks, honor, and glory as before. The day came as I lay in bed, I saw Him. His arms were folded, as a king would fold his arms, and His great eyes looked right through me. His legs and feet were as great wheels the size of a small Ferris wheel, spinning faster than 100 miles per hour, as a wheel in the middle of a wheel (Eze. 1:16). His overall expression was as one who was prepared for war. My God was there, right in front of me, seemingly suspended between Heaven and earth. Beneath His feet, I saw nations, oceans, a multitude of people, storms, winds, and cities. I was speechless. Suddenly, He spoke firm words of chastisement into my heart without opening His mouth, saying: "*You wanted to see Me, My son; here I am. Go forth and do not tarry. I have given you your assignment, obey Me and fulfill all My will.*" Because I was gifted, chosen, called, and anointed for God's purpose, I knew this personal visitation and divine experience with Him was serious and there would also be a confrontation with Satan, God's arch enemy, who is a heart thief (Lk. 8:11), a heart filler (Acts 5:1-4), molester, and a/the deceiver. Yet by God's visitation and presence I was encouraged. I knew the Lord was with me

Several months passed by, and one morning as I lay upon my bed, Satan came into my room, crawling upon the ceiling as a great serpent (snake), saying: "*I am Satan, and you will not be able to do all the things that you plan to do.*" I reminded him how the Lord had defeated him on Calvary over 2,000 years ago. I felt no fear, and as I began to rebuke and bind him at his heart in *Jesus'* name, he quickly did exit out my window and crashed into an <u>outhouse</u> outside. Immediately all trees, plants, grass, and other vegetation turned white and became lifeless and hard (petrified) as a stone. I heard his voice again, saying the same thing, and I responded the same way, commanding him to flee in Jesus' name. I prayed and anointed my house with oil, asking the Lord for understanding. He spoke into my spirit, saying: "*Do not fear him, My son, but obey My voice. Observe the place he ran into.*" I kept a smile upon my face for several days, knowing Satan, the god of roaches, mice and flies, was also the lord of every outhouse (Don's johns). I realized that Satan has not had a bath (cleansing) for thousands of years since he was cast out of heaven. By this time, I had written several books on the heart (*Hidden Treasures of the Heart, Code Red: Wars of the Heart,* and *Code Blue: Serious Matters of the Heart*). Satan sent his first hindering spirit to hinder my coming to *The Heart of the Cross* message. Early one morning as I lay asleep in my bed, I felt my bed almost sink to the floor. I awoke to see a great black demonic spirit leaning over me with forked hands that pinned me to the bed so I couldn't move or breathe. I was wide-awake. Habitually, I keep my television on a gospel channel all night long. As I began to call on the Lord, to my surprise so did the preacher who was preaching on the television. Together at the same time we began to bind Satan at his heart, and I began to bind the demon holding me captive. Faster than my eyes could see, he jumped from my bed onto my computer table, turned into a great dragon, and disappeared into thin air. In every confrontation I've had with Satan and his kingdom of darkness, fear was their greatest weapon used against me. Yet none cause me more concern as the one I call mammon, **the green money demon**.

In a vision, I saw myself teaching a Bible class in my home, in my den where there was a very large picture window. There were about fifteen students and one of them spoke out loud unto me, saying: "Excuse me, teacher, but did you know there was a storm warning about a tornado coming this way?" Being concerned, I went to my large picture window, and to my surprise there was a great tornado coming directly toward my house, about a block away. It was huge, terrible, black, with all kinds of items within it such as automobiles, trucks, people, houses, train boxcars; it was such a horrible sight. With fear, I shouted for everyone to run down into the basement for shelter and to get into a corner and to take cover. As my house began to disintegrate (come apart), out of the great tornado came a green colored beast. It was at least eight feet tall and made of $100 bills. He walked through my closed door, looked intently at me, and said: "I have come for you, to ordain you with money as my servant in secret." Immediately there stood beside me an angel of God, saying: "*Do not be afraid of him, I am not afraid of him. Do not compromise with him, for he is mammon.*" She (my guardian angel) stood at least nine feet tall and was there for my protection and safety. Suddenly, mammon (Satan's servant in disguise) stretched forth a long, skinny, feeble arm to lay it upon me and ordain me as his servant in secret. My angel from God never ceased speaking to me and warning me that mammon is evil, a liar, deceiver, a destroyer, and not to be afraid. The Spirit of God rose up within me with power, and ever so boldly I began to plead the blood of the cross against him. I awoke and made a vow never to compromise God's Word, but to tell the truth from my heart, with all my heart, and to warn all about the Spirit of Mammon, even though at that time I never knew who mammon really was. I thanked God that He had sent an angel to watch over me.

For several months I could not get the incident out of my heart and mind. Knowing Satan is a liar, deceiver, imitator, and a god of this world, I began to search for scriptures. I found out God had not given us a spirit of fear (2 Tim. 1:7), He took Elijah into Heaven by a whirlwind (2 Kgs. 2:1-11), He also spoke to Job out of a whirlwind

(Job 38:1), and He has a whirlwind (Jer. 23:19, 30:23 and Eze. 1:3-5). Just as the Lord stood by the Apostle Paul and gave him strength (2 Tim. 4:17), He stood by me that day, His angel giving me strength and divine instructions.

I later found out the green money monster had the biblical name of Mammon, an Aramaic word for riches. Christ describes him in Matthew 6:24 as a master (god) of money. In Luke 16:9, 11 and 13 he is all unrighteousness. No one can carry their cross and serve mammon at the same time. Yet I knew if I would serve mammon in secret, he would provide me with money, wealth, illegal sex, drugs, and fame. As I made a deeper commitment to serve the Lord as His servant, he began to draw me closer to writing this book, *The Heart of the Cross*.

The Cross Within My Doctor's Office

Like most folks, I do not care much for doctor appointments, yet I had one and was running about fifteen minutes late. As I rushed into his office, a kind nurse took me into a private room, saying the doctor would be with me shortly. As I sat there waiting for him, I happened to look down at the floor, and what I saw was a large cross deep inside of the floor. I was stunned and surprised. I began to pray, worship, and thank the Lord for His <u>finished work</u> on Calvary. When the doctor came into the room, he began to speak to me in a very professional manner and introduced himself to me, but I interrupted him, saying: "Doctor, do you see what is there within your floor?" His finger pointed at the cross and he asked, "Why, what is that?" Since he was from another country, I explained the Cross of Jesus Christ to him. With eyes wide open and staring at the cross, he stated how that room had been in his office for over fourteen years and he had never seen anything like that. Suddenly the cross was gone. For the next few months, I went through scriptures concerning the cross, seeking to gain more information and revelation from God about the cross in order to write this book.

The Man Beneath The Cross

Our God is new every morning, and one morning as I was driving my car, I saw in my spirit Jesus Christ hanging on the cross. Beneath Him was a man standing looking intently up at Him. Both were surrounded by morning mist, so I was unable to see them clearly. I thought how I had seen many pictures of Jesus on Calvary, but never one with someone standing beneath Him. The vision went away. Later that day it came back again, and this time when I looked at the man who stood beneath the Lord, I recognized who the man was. To my surprise, that man was me! All of my emotions came alive, love met with passion as my heart caused tears to flow like rain. I began crying like a small child when I realized that even if I were the only lost sinner in the earth, Jesus would have still come forward to die for me and all my sins. Not only did He give His life for all, He also gave His heart. "What a great Heart You have, my Lord!" I cried out to Him and began to thank and praise Him with all of my heart, soul and strength.

The revelation that hit me to my heart and soul, searing my mind as a hot iron, was when I realized in all the years of teaching and preaching the Gospel of the Heart, I never saw the heart of Jesus as He hung there on Calvary. I had seen His bruised, bloody and beaten body, but never His heart. The Lord had me standing beneath Him, looking up at His kind, forgiving and loving heart. Immediately I realized as soon as the vision went away, any godly message given to man is the message that's from God's Heart, *The Heart of the Cross*. I knew I must write a book using this title, to also write about the heart of God as they crucified His only begotten Son, the heart of the two thieves, the hearts of those who nailed Him to the Cross, and the people who stood by watching, enraged, and cursing at Him. In addition to this, none did discern His magnificent, eminent, and glorious mind.

My journey to *The Heart of the Cross* has caused me to look more closely at the three crosses: The Cross of Jesus Christ, the cross of the two thieves, and our cross that we must take up daily to follow Him (Lk. 9:23-25 and 14:25-27). The heart is our power and vehicle wherein we carry our cross made by the hands of God. Our hearts will always express themselves to others around us, even directly to another heart. It may walk (follow) after the eyes (Job 31:7), or after abominations and detestable things (Eze. 11:21).

On May 5, 2019, as I sat watching television, a music video for the music icon named Prince came on. He was very loud, yet the musicians were great, as were the people around him doing outstanding dance routines. He played his guitar and danced like James Brown and Michael Jackson. I couldn't help but notice the cross he had imprinted upon the left side of his face and the large heart printed on the back of his shirt. But the thing that impacted me the most was the song he was singing. In the midst of the fire, smoke, and funky rock music, he was singing about *the Cross of Jesus Christ* with lyrics such as: *"Don't die without knowing the cross,"* *"we will have bread if we bear the cross,"* and *"our problems will be taken by the cross."* At the very end of the video were the words, *"All thanks be to God!"* I crossed my heart and with a made-up mind, I decided to write this book and share with the world and every church group the great news about *The Heart of the Cross*.

Chapter 8
Body Parts That Affect Every Believer's Heart

Now that we have come to deeper revelation of *The Heart of the Cross*, here are some very important parts of our bodies that are fully and firmly heart-connected and operated. I'm speaking of the eyes that see, our mouths that speak, lips that entice, the tongue that rules and the ears that hear. These are as great highways, byways, and pathways both to and from our hearts, and do have a direct influence upon our souls and minds. Being both natural and spiritual they rule within our lives and affect all we see, say and do, our salvation, cross life, cross connection, prayer life, and our intimate relationship with God.

The Eyes

Eyes are vision, sight, and perception, the means with which we view, observe, watch, and behold. In Genesis, God reveals He also has eyes to see, for He saw all His works were good (Gen. 1:31). Satan came into the Garden of Eden, speaking to Eve negative words and lies to deceive her. She saw the forbidden tree was good to look at, and she ate of it, as well as Adam. *"And the eyes of them both were opened, and they knew that they were naked; and they sewed fig leaves together and made themselves aprons"* (Gen. 3:7). We learn from this that Satan defiled, deceived, and influenced the lives and hearts of Adam and Eve. What they saw and ate was the primary cause of their disobedience to God. In 2 Kings 6:8-20, the Prophet Elijah and his servant were surrounded by their enemies. He asked God to open the eyes of his servant to see they were safe. God opened the servant's spiritual eyes and he saw. The Lord opens the eyes of the blind (Ps. 146:8). The eyes have a profound effect upon the heart (Lam. 3:51). There can be nothing more harmful and hindering than sin and the blindness of our hearts and eyes (Eph. 4:17-18). Jesus warned us of those blind leaders who lead the blind (Matt. 15:14). The Apostle Paul in Acts 28:27 saw the seriousness of this problem, and speaking by the Holy Spirit said this: *"For the heart of this people is become obtuse* (dull, slow to understand or perceive), *and their ears are dull of hearing, and their eyes they have closed; lest they should <u>see with their eyes</u> and hear with their ears, and understand with their hearts and be converted and I should heal them."* (See also Matt. 6:22-23) But we see Jesus, who was made a little lower than the angels for the suffering of death, crowned with glory and honor, that He, by the grace of God, should taste death for every man (Heb. 2:9).

We must always see clearly by the eyes of our understanding and be governed by an understanding heart (Eph. 1:18 and 1 Kgs. 3:9). The eyes may cry tears (Is. 38:5), they may wink at others (Pr. 6:13 and 10:10), and yet be evil (Mk. 7:22). Our hearts may walk after the eyes (Job 31:7). The eyes of the Lord search the whole earth looking for perfect hearts (2 Chron. 16:9). The eyes of Jesus Christ cried tears (Lk. 19:41-42 and John 11:32-35). Tears speak words that our mouths cannot always express. In Psalm 34:8, the great psalmist David gave us excellent instruction, saying: "*Oh, taste and '<u>see</u>'* (discern, behold, observe and understand) *that the Lord is good; blessed is the man who trusteth in Him.*" We look unto God and the cross that we might see the right way to know His perfect will, ways, word, and works. The wisdom of Proverbs 16:9 reveals that a man's heart devises (plans, regulates) his way (eyesight), but the Lord directs (conducts) his steps. We know we are truly blessed when we have spiritual eyes to see (Matt. 13:13-17). Without seeing eyes, there is serious blindness of our hearts (Eph. 4:18). Jesus turned to His disciples privately and said: "*Blessed are the eyes which see the things that you see*" (Lk. 10:23-24). Good natural and spiritual eyesight are so important. In the great waters of the sea, God has given the smart octopus eight legs, two hearts, and one great eye to see. When the Lord returns, we shall see His glory, His nail-scarred hands, even those who pierced Him in His side, drove the nails into His hands and the thorns into His head. Every eye shall see Him (Jn. 19:37 and Rev. 1:7).

The Mouth

The mouth is our oral opening and cavity, a portal, outlet, and inlet. Our facial orifice that contains the lips and tongue wherein we speak, say, declare, shape our words, and utter our voice. If our hearts condemn us (1 Jn. 3:20-21) it will be because of the words of our mouths. Jesus warned us, saying: *"But I say unto you that every idle (pointless, futile, vain, empty) word that men shall speak, they shall give account of it in the Day of Judgment. For by thy words thou shall be condemned"* (Matt. 12:36-37). (See also Lk. 6:45 and Matt. 12:33-35) Again, the Lord spoke concerning the mouth and how we should live: *"And the devil said unto Him, if thou be the Son of God, command this stone that it be made bread. And Jesus answered him saying, It is written, man shall not live by bread alone, but by every word that proceedeth out of the mouth of God"* (Lk. 4:3-4). (See also Deut. 8:1-3, Rom. 10:8-10 and Rev. 3:15-20)

In all the earth, especially in the church there is an emergency need for **Mouth Control**. Our mouths are the greatest snare for our souls (Pr. 6:2). We all need mouth control more than we need money (Pr. 13:3) (See also Acts 28:23-29). Out of the heart the mouth speaks. For this we need God's Word in our hearts so we do not sin against God with our mouths (Ps. 119:11, Jer. 20:8-9 and Pr. 4:4). Yet we must be fully aware that our hearts don't need mouths to speak unto others. We need a right heart for right words and a right mouth, for a right life in godliness and righteousness. Nothing can be more harmful for our ear-gate than a mouth-gate speaking wrong and hurtful words

The Tongue

The organ of speech, vocabulary, organ of taste, a movable muscle within the mouth, and the power of speech. In my book, ***The Pen of a Ready Writer***, I was inspired when David in Psalm 45:1 stated: *"My heart is overflowing with a good matter; my tongue is the pen of a ready writer."* It was revealed to me that the tongue has the power to write things upon the hearts and minds of others (Ps. 39:1 and 52:1-5). Like the heart, it may be deceitful (Mic. 6:12). It may confess to God (Rom. 14:11 and Phil. 2:10). The wisdom of Proverbs 18:20-21 warns us with great emphasis concerning the tongue, saying: *"A man's belly (heart) shall be satisfied with the fruit of his mouth, and with the increase of his lips he shall be filled. Death and life are in the power of the tongue, and they that love it shall eat the fruit thereof."* The ignorant stick out their tongues in <u>mockery</u> to ridicule, deride, mimic, and make fun of. The tongue may be used to even provoke, scorn, be rude, and make insulting remarks about one with humiliating facts. It is the prime organ (culprit) of <u>backbiting</u> that's often connected to a lie or word abuse that kills or destroys relationships, marriages, and church families. A backbiting tongue is hurtful, firmly connected to gossip that reduces and disassembles. Let us paraphrase James 3:1-10 that we may see the importance of mouth control and putting bridles upon our tongues, as they do to horses to control them (See also Jms. 1:26).

Even though the tongue is a little member, it is a great controlling fire, a world of iniquity (immorality, evil, sin, wrong, injustice). A great defiling power that corrupts, pollutes, contaminates, and disgraces the whole body. It may direct our nature and lead us directly into the fires of hell. While mankind has tamed great lions, elephants, snakes, and dogs, yet no man can tame the evil tongue that's full of deadly poison. God's presence in our hearts along with His love, word, and Holy Spirit are more than capable of keeping our tongues in order.

The Lips

Our lips are the overlapping portal of speech, a nozzle, a speech organ that is located at the edge of the mouth. It is a fleshly portion at the edge of the mouth that acts as a spout or flange. Like unto our hearts, eyes, and mouth, our lips may speak unto others without words. In the book of Job 2:9-10, we read about Job's terrible tragedies and yet the scripture states that: *"in all of this Job did not sin with his lips."* Just as the tongue and mouth may utter lies, there is nothing more deceitful than *lying lips*. As we guard our hearts, we must put far away from us a crooked mouth and perverse (wicked, obstinate, contrary, erring) lips (Pr. 4:23-24). (See also Pr. 12:13-22, 16:23-25 and Rom. 3:9-18)

In Mark 7:5-7, Jesus spoke to the religious leaders as they sought to condemn Him: *"Well has Isaiah prophesied of our hypocrites; as it is written. This people honoreth me with their lips, but their heart is far from me. However in vain do they worship me, teaching for doctrines the commandments of men."* To avoid useless lips of worship and far away hearts, all church leaders must make sure as they open the doors of the local church that the Lord is the first one to enter. Lips also have their power and fame in a kiss. Judas betrayed Jesus with a kiss of his lips as a signal for the soldiers to come take Jesus and crucify Him. Judas, with Satan in his heart (Lk. 22:3), said, "Hail, Master," and kissed Him. Then they laid their hands upon the Lord and took Him into prison and onward unto His cross (Matt. 26:47-50) to be crucified. Most assuredly, lips can act as a snare (trap, lure, deception) for our very souls (Pr. 18:6-7).

The Ears

The ears are our organ of hearing, a canal, acoustic auditory apparatus, and perception of sound. A listening device and projection with three basic parts called the outer ear, the middle ear, and the inner ear. Being both natural and spiritual, they influence the eyes and mouth, and also determine our hearts' response. They give us the ability to recognize the difference in sounds, especially God's voice, the voice of leaders and loved ones, even the many voices of devils and demons. Jesus said this: *"Behold, I stand at the door and knock; If any man hear my voice I will come in to him, and will sup* (dine) *with him, and he with me"* (Rev. 3:20). While the eyes may cause the mouth to speak, the ears may cause the heart to respond. We hear (h-ear) from our heart (h-ear-t) and we want God to hear our cry, prayers, and our voices with His ears (2 Kgs. 19:16, Ps. 34:15 and 54:2). It is God who gives us eyes to see and ears to hear (Deut. 29:4). From musical tones to God's Word unto the common sounds of the earth, ears give us power to hear speech, to spiritually listen to our very own hearts and to hear what mouths (tongue and lips) are saying.

Job 34:1-3 teaches us that ears test (inspect, analyze, inquire, search, examine) words as the mouth tastes food. God's voice has gone out among the nations, saying *"Hear Ye O Israel"* (Mk. 12:29). (See also Rom. 10:14-17 and 11:8) He knows our ears may be dull of hearing (Acts 28:26-27 and Heb. 5:11). On His way to Calvary, not only did He cast out devils, heal the sick of their infirmities and plagues, and give sight to the blind, but He caused the deaf to hear. He said unto them: *"Go your way and tell John* (the Baptist) *what things you have seen and heard -- how the blind see, the lame walk, the leapers are cleansed,* **the deaf hear***, the dead are raised, to the poor the gospel is preached"* (Lk. 7:21-22). (See also Is. 35:3-6, 43:48 and Mk. 7:37) *"Woe unto those who are uncircumcised in heart and ears"* (Acts 7:51). (See also Jer. 7:23-26, Rom. 2:25-29 and Col. 2:9-13) But as it is written, eye has not seen, nor ear heard, neither have entered into the hearts of men the things God has prepared for those who love Him (1 Cor. 2:9). Rest assured that by *The Heart of the Cross,* God is well able through Jesus

Christ to give us pure and clean mouths, holy eyes that clearly see, and clean <u>ears to hear</u> His Rhema word. "Blessed are they that hear the Word of God and keep it" (Lk. 11:28). (Matt. 13:13-23)

Chapter 9
The Forensics Of A Heavenly Heart

Forensics are commonplace in the earth and have been used by law enforcement agencies wherever there is a crime, robbery, murder, deadly accident, or the need for accurate information to determine the cause or guilty person(s). Forensics also include the medical field and government agencies worldwide. They perform a forensic search of a place, event, and every article of importance to know the truth of what happened, "who done it," and what is really there.

Most certainly we need natural forensics to be in place, but the greater importance is the forensics of our spiritual hearts, an investigation and study of our hearts using God's Word as an instrument to know our hearts' contents, condition, value, and importance. Now is the season to investigate and observe our heart theology and topography that involve spiritual cardiology that our natural eyes can't see, and to know our spiritual hearts, their size, position, contents, and condition by an accurate detailed forensic description.

Fervently, God wants us to know what He knows about us. Forensic heart topography gives us more accurate information, better education, greater knowledge and revelation, that we may be all we are supposed to be within our hearts, our hidden man of the heart (1 Pet. 3:4). For Christians to become heaven-ready, all must come to the epitome of *kardiognostees*, which is a knower of hearts, and like unto the Lord, knowing all that can be known of both our natural and spiritual hearts. This is because: "*the heart is deceitful* (dishonest, cunning, tricky) *above all things and desperately* (dangerously, harmfully, seriously) *wicked* (evil, corrupt). *Who can know it? I the Lord search the heart, and test* (try) *the conscience* (reins) *even to give every one according to his ways, and according to the fruit of his doings.*" (Jer. 17:9-10) He knows our hearts' forensics (Acts 1:24 and 15:8). While we have given thanks and praises to David for giving unto us Psalm 23:1-6, we have grossly neglected his forensic cry and prayer to God, which is most needful today for God's approval of our heavenly hearts. "*Search me, O God, and know my heart; try me, and know my thoughts; and see if there be any wicked way in me, and lead me in the way everlasting*" (Ps. 139:23-24). His asking God to do a forensic search analysis of his heart may have come from his passionate desire for God to cleanse or replace his heart due to uncleanness, and his personal assessment of himself. "*Purge me with hyssop, and I shall be clean; wash me, and I shall be whiter than snow. Create in me a clean heart, O God, and renew a right spirit within me*" (Ps. 51:7-9, 10).

The greatest forensic event to ever take place upon the Earth was/is the *Heart of the Cross* of Jesus Christ . That was a <u>crime scene</u> because He was not guilty, yet they crucified Him; it was a *sin scene* because innocently He took upon Himself the sin (and sins) of this world, past, present, and future. Yet it was a great victory scene wherein Christ won the victory over death, hell, and the grave for us. God revealed the forensics of the cross unto the Prophet Isaiah, approximately 800 years before it actually happened. He prophesied and wrote that Christ's visage (face, features, profile, appearance, and image) was marred more than any man and His form more than the sons of men. He was smitten of God, afflicted, wounded for our transgressions, bruised, and beaten with thirty-nine stripes and carried all of our iniquities unto death (Is. 52:14 and 53:3-12). The sin scene of the cross forensics is the fact that He was despised and rejected of men and numbered with the wicked that we may be changed, saved, filled with heavenly hearts, and heaven-ready.

To be sure of our destiny and condition of our heavenly hearts, I recommend we consider these things:

A Forensic Heart Investigation: A review, inquiry study, to inspect, examine closely, exploratory survey and scan for validity, error, flaws, and preparation. This is important because we do not need the Lord our God to be on the outside of us looking in, but on the inside of our hearts, looking out. He may be on our minds, but it's mandatory for salvation for Him to be there in our hearts. The hard drive of our minds must be directly connected to the website of our hearts, so that whenever sin, evil thoughts or ungodly imaginations come, no weapon shall overcome us. Many Christians and leaders wear expensive clothing, drive $50,000 cars, live in million-dollar homes, while having $10 hearts within. Bad hearts act up, but good hearts act out. Men are counting bodies in ministry, but God is counting hearts.

There Has to be Evidence: A testimony, looking for proof, facts, confirmation, grounds for our belief, visible signs and unmistakable data that we are who we confess to be. This is because our hearts may speak to God while we're asleep. (Ps. 27:8) It is with our hearts we believe (Rom. 10:11). Out of our hearts flow the issues of life (Pr. 4:20-23). Most all seek God for forgiveness of sins but have forgotten to seek Him for the forgiveness of their evil thoughts and wicked imaginations (Acts 8:17-22). A distant heart will/can never walk with the Lord (Is. 29:13 and Mk. 7:5-9). When we celebrate Christmas, let us not forget to give the Lord the one gift He wants most of all, which is our hearts. (Pr. 23:26)

We Must Have Correct Heart Information: Heart analysis, assessment, knowledge of, disclosure, news, and proof. For correct results, the forensics of the mind and its renewal status must be observed. A renewed mind works best when there is a set heart committed and given to God. Satan loves to see a church on Sunday that's full of empty hearts. Where there are empty seats, the problem is often empty hearts. As we travel along the many pathways of life, we should always make our hearts the first stop. The type of sin, crime, wrong things we do and the life we live are fully predicated upon the type of hearts that lie within us. In the midst of racism (color separation), man looks upon the color of one's skin and not the forensics, state or condition of the mind and heart. A racist heart can never ascend unto a heavenly heart status. It is so very foolish for any race of people to gain the whole world and lose their own souls forever.

Heavenly Hearts

I believe the birthing and giving of heavenly hearts from God unto man came into full power, blessings and glory by the *Heart of the Cross* of Jesus Christ. By His death, burial and resurrection, every type of heart God intended for mankind to have (or would ever need) was firmly set in place, position and power, to rule the Earth, be seated in God's presence, in heavenly places, God's kingdom, forever ruling in authority over Satan's kingdom of ungodly and hellish hearts. Before the cross, Old Testament forensics and knowledge of heavenly hearts was very rare, seldom seen or known, being under the law and commandments until the cross of Christ. For God to fix man's sin issues, the powers of darkness and death, He must first fix man's heart, the power, root, source and issue of life.

A heavenly heart may be identified as one that is excellent, God-approved, and well able to take us into God's kingdom, to the abode of the blessed, God's throne in glory, our eternal home, and final resting place. A heavenly heart is mightily used of God, known by Him, and is His dwelling place in the earth. It is separate from sin, we have the victory, our salvation is complete, and our names are written in the Lamb's book of Life. A heavenly heart in the midst of trials, troubles, heavy burdens, sin sickness and woe, will worship the Lord, giving thanks, praise and glory, knowing Jesus Christ has won the victory for us. While there is no greater blessing in all the Earth than having a heavenly heart to guide us through this life, we must beware and be wise concerning our enemies that I will namely call "Satan's Hellish Hearts," who go to and fro throughout the Earth, seeking to kill, steal and destroy.

Other prime enemies of our heavenly hearts are all sin, the love of money, wrong words, doubt and unbelief, false religion, man's doctrine, pride, rebelliousness, disobedience, lack of knowledge and wasted time. Let us view seven types of heavenly hearts that I believe are mandatory for eternal life. Daily forensic observance is highly recommended.

A Loving Heart = A heart that is full of compassion, kindness, grace, mercy and the Lord Jesus Christ. It is a tender heart, very affectionate, caring, passionate and true. It took Jesus to the cross and will receive all other hearts unto itself in glory. (Deut. 6:5, 30:6, Mk. 12:28-33, Jn. 5:5-8 and 1 Pet. 1:22)

A Believing Heart = A heart that is full of faith and trust in God and His Word. It is confident, hope-filled, with great expectation and the strength of our salvation. (Acts. 8:35-37, and Rom. 10:9-11.) See faith(ful) heart. (Neh. 9:8) See a trusting heart. (Pr. 3:5 and Ps. 28:7)

A New Heart = A different heart. Fresh. Unspoiled. Uncontaminated. Unique and brand new. (Eze. 18:31 and 26:25-26) Blessed with a new heart covenant. (Heb. 8:8-10 and 10:14-18)

A Repentant Heart = A heart that's pricked by the Holy Spirit and given to God. (Acts 2:36-38) One that is sorry, regretful for sins and wrong, remorseful and apologetic. (Mk. 1:4, Acts 8:22 and Rom. 2:4) One that says yes to God's will and word, and no to sin and all wrong.

A Holy Heart = A sacred, sinless, godly, moral and virtuous heart. One that is sanctified, faithful and true. (1 Pet. 1:15-16, 1 Thess. 3:18 and Heb. 12:14) It sits upon the throne of obedience and is God-approved.

A Perfect Heart = A great heart, one that's genuine, complete, excellent, sound, made whole, flawless, sinless, immaculate and helps us to stand in the likeness and image of God. (1 Kgs. 8:61, 1 Chron. 28:9, Is. 38:3, and Matt. 5:48) God's expectation is perfection. A heart that's God-filled, word-filled, faith-filled, and love overflowing. He is able. (2 Tim. 3:17) Note: Jesus has not built an <u>imperfect church</u> (Matt 16:18), neither is there found <u>in Christ</u> an imperfect heart.

A Pure and Clean Heart = A heart that's pure, meaning it is real, true, genuine, spotless, and complete, to mean one that is immaculate, chaste, disinfected, purified and washed by the blood of the cross (Ps. 24:4, Matt. 5:8, 1 Pet. 1:22) and clean (Ps. 51:7-10). A blessed heart, wherein God makes "heart deposits" daily, and says: Well done, My good and faithful servant.

Because heavenly hearts are infinite, they require things that are eternal, God-made and blessed, such as the Word of God (Ps. 119:11, Jer. 20:9, and Lk. 8:11-12). They are far too precious to be full of worldly riches and drawn by the lust of the eyes, flesh, and the pride of life. They respond to the name of Jesus, giving honor, glory, thanksgiving and hallelujahs all the day long. They will seek and search out God's great heart to know His will, word, plans, desires and mighty power. These hearts will always take us to the King and to eternal glory through *The Heart of the Cross*. Though they are a blessing, we do not always discern their need and the inner wars they must fight, even thoughts and imaginations of our minds that may cause them to become weak, in need of rest, repair, and help from the Lord. He has seven extra hearts that are well able to come forth unto their aid and rescue, and lead them to Heaven's doors.

Saved Hearts that Strengthen Heavenly Hearts

A Right Heart = A righteous heart that's upright before God and man. Honest, just, lawful, valid, correct and straight. Makes us worthy before God and trustworthy before man. Virtuous, good, guiltless and reliable. (2 Kgs. 10:15 and Acts 8:18-22) (For a non-right heart, Ps. 78:37)

A Praying Heart = A heart that asks, entreats and petitions God, calling on God with an earnest request. A devout heart that's full of devotion, supplication, thanksgiving and appeal. (2 Sam. 7:27 and 1 Chron. 17:25) The joy of this heart is answered prayer. (1 Sam. 2:1)

A Word-Filled Heart = This heart is full of God's biblical utterances. The heart of Jesus Christ was/is Word-filled. It is the Lord speaking from His dwelling place in us and through us unto all other hearts and upon the Earth, both saved and unsaved. A glorious heart full of power and God's presence. (Ps. 119:11 and Job 22:21)

A Forgiven (and Forgiving) Heart = God by His grace and mercy uses this heart (even His own heart) to show His love and kindness to every lost sinner and born again believer. A heart that leads in God's salvation plan. Every heavenly heart gives honor and praise for this heart of God, that's been pardoned, excused of all wrong, justified and reinstated. (Acts 8:22, Eph. 4:32, Col. 3:13 and 1 Jn. 1:9)

A Wise and Understanding Heart = A wise heart is intelligent, perceptive, knowing and of good judgment. A heart of discernment, comprehension and understanding. It may also function as an understanding heart wherein it has additional power of insight, sensitivity and intuition to grasp what we must say and do as believers at the right time and place. (Ex. 28:3, 1 Kgs. 3:9 and 12, Ps. 49:3 and Pr. 23:15)

A Prepared (and Established) Heart = A prepared heart will soon establish itself in God through Jesus Christ. It is a heart that stands in a ready position to do God's work, will and pleasure. It has been put in order, perfected, fully developed, built up, qualified and equipped. (1 Sam. 7:3, Ps. 10:17, and Pr. 16:1) It promotes a godly lifestyle. A believer is quickly established in the gospel of Jesus Christ, which means to be planted, built, settled, rooted, unshakeable, authenticated, validated and proven. (Ps. 112:8, 1 Thess. 3:13, and Jms. 5:8)

Heavenly hearts are saved hearts that will never allow true born again believers to depart from God's presence. They will always take us to godliness, holiness, worship, truth, prayer, to read and obey God's Word. Giving thanks, glory, praise, and honor unto God, we find favor and blessings beyond measure. In these last and evil days, the *Heart of the Cross* represents every type of heart that exists upon the face of the earth. Because the Lord doesn't want any heart or life to be lost, Christ died that all hearts and souls may be saved. Yet there are two kingdoms of hearts that we may freely choose: the kingdom of darkness ruled by Satan and the kingdom of light ruled by our Lord and Savior, Jesus Christ. In Matthew 7:13-14, He makes reference to both, saying: *"Enter in at the strait (narrow) gate; for wide is the gate, and broad is the way that leads to destruction, and many there be who go in that way; because straight (narrow) is the gate, and hard (unyielding, firm) is the way, which leadeth unto life and few there be that find it."* Because heart forensics determine both Heaven and Hell, let us now view some of the hellish hearts and their forensics that work all evil, sin, crime, wickedness, wrongdoing, death and hell in both this world and the local assembly.

The Forensics and Kingdom of Hellish Hearts

Hellish hearts are those that are dead to God's will, word, plans, purpose and the gospel of Jesus Christ. They are prime enemies of the cross of Christ (Phil. 3:18-20). They are all devilish, unclean, Satan's glory design, diabolical, disobedient haters of God, man, and each other. They are enemies and haters of Heaven. All are bad, worthless, and shall never walk eternally in heavenly places. (Matt. 23:24-28 and 33, Lk. 16:4-19 and 2 Pet. 2:4-5) They had their beginning when Satan was cast out of Heaven because of his heart's desire to rule over God, His throne and kingdom (Is. 14:12-14).

An Evil Heart = A heart that's immoral, wicked, sinful, bad, wrong, sinister, vile, foul, destructive, the ultimate power of iniquity and corruption. (Gen. 6:5-6, 8:21, Matt. 9:4 and Mk. 7:21-23)

A Deceitful Heart = A heart that's dishonest, very cunning, deceptive, insincere, sneaky and loving to lie. From con artists to swindlers and from hypocrites to fraudulent persons, the deceitful heart is at work. (Deut. 11:16, Pr. 12:20, Jer. 17:9-10, Rom. 16:18 and Js. 1:26) It works together with a lying heart.

A Rebellious (and Disobedient) Heart = While rebellious hearts are mostly Old Testament, of men who were unruly, defiant, and disorderly (Jer. 5:20-24), the New Testament uses the word disobedient for anyone who is stubborn, not submissive, haughty, perverse, and obstinate (Eph. 2:2, Col. 3:6, Tit. 1:16, 3:3 and 1 Pet. 2:7-8). Both are overall interchangeable.

An Unclean (and Defiled) Heart = A heart unclean is one that's morally impure, vile, filthy, nasty, soiled, and maggoty. As one of Satan's favorite hearts (he is also unclean), being defiled is polluted, contaminated, dirty, debased, and corrupt. (Matt. 23:25-28, Mk. 7:6-7, 20, 23, and Eph. 5:5)

A Hard (and Stony) Heart = A hard heart is one that is cruel, unfeeling, uncaring, merciless, cold, inhuman, ruthless and insensitive (Mk. 16:14, 3:5, and Jn. 12:40). In its attributes, hardness and character, it is known as a stony heart, one that's stubborn, ugly, harmful, unkind, vindictive, brutal, merciless and vicious (Eze. 11:19, 36:26, and Matt. 13:3-9 and 15-23). Israel was hardhearted (Eze. 3:7). The Lord was grieved by the hardness of His disciples' hearts (Mk. 3:5 and 16:14).

A Lying Heart = The power behind every lie. A heart full of untruth, falsehood, misinformation, deception, fabrication, distortion, delusion, forgery and inaccuracy. It rules in man's false religion, all ungodliness and sinful lifestyles. As a prime enemy of faith, salvation, truth, righteousness, and belief, Satan works as the liar and father of lies (Jn. 8:44 and 55, Acts 5:3, 2 Thess. 2:9, Eph. 4:25 and Rev. 21:8)

An Unbelieving Heart = This is a heart that's full of doubt, skepticism, disbelief and uncertainty. It has its place in skeptics, atheists, and people who call themselves free thinkers. In every religion that doubts the Lord Jesus Christ is God's Son, there is a heart of unbelief. Doubt (mistrust, lack of faith, and being uncertain) causes many to be lost to God's heavenly throne of grace. Doubt and unbelief do contaminate the heart and work as blood clots within the spiritual heart of man. (2 Cor. 6:14, Heb. 3:12-19) (For doubt, see Mk. 11:23 and Lk. 12:29)

Forensics of Lost Hearts that Support Hellish Hearts

There are many souls upon the Earth that are dead while they yet live (Lk. 9:59-60). Being spiritually dead to God in their hearts, and yet breathing and alive is a very suspicious thing. The Lord in His love and grace may perform a spiritual autopsy upon their dead hearts and spirits to determine if a heart transplant is needed.

The word autopsy means a seeing with one's own eyes to discover the cause of death or damage done by sin or rebelliousness. Being the "living dead," they give full support to every hellish heart.

A Lustful (and Whorish) Heart = Hearts found in people having their appetite and passion for pleasure out of control. Full of wanting, sexual desire, longing, and hunger. They are sensual, extremely carnal, bound in concupiscence. (Matt 5:27-28, Rom. 1:24-27, Jms. 1:14-15) For the whorish hearts, the love of money is the issue in their life of whoredom, and they are known as harlots and whoremongers. (Pr. 6:25-26, Eze. 6:9, Eph. 5:5, 1 Tim. 1:10, Heb. 13:4 and Rev. 21:8) From pornography to child molestation, and from rape unto family incest, this heart is fervently at work. It is also seen in the love of money, which is the root of all evil (Jms. 6:9-10).

A Foolish Heart = A heart that is unwise, silly, senseless, overall stupid and absurd, causing its victims to act irrationally, idiotically, crazily, without good sense as a moron or ignoramus. A Simple Simon, scatterbrain, birdbrain or a clown. (Ps. 53:1, Pr. 12:23, 15:7, Lk. 12:15-21, 24:25, and Rom. 1:21) A fool's heart may say that there is no God, no Hell to go to, and that same-sex marriage is God-approved.

A Backsliding (and Departing) Heart = A backsliding heart is one that regresses, has turned around from God, reversed, has broken the faith, fallen from grace, and exists in an apostatized state. (Pr. 14:14, Jer. 3:6-24, 7:24, and Hos. 11:7) As a departing heart it has turned aside from following God and has made its exit from grace. (Jer. 17:5, Eze. 6:9, and Heb. 3:12)

A Proud (Prideful) Heart = A proud heart is one that's egotistic, arrogant, haughty, conceited, vain and boastful. It is exalted in self-reliance, self-sufficient self-respecting and pleased with itself. (Ps. 101:5, Pr. 16:5, 21:4, 28:25 and 1 Pet. 5:5) While being proud of what is good and honorable is acceptable, believers must not allow their hearts to become full of pride, wherein they become conceited, self-loved, self-esteemed as Satan did in Heaven and was cast out. A prideful heart of self-exaltation, self-esteem and complacency will soon forget God. (Pr. 16:18, Is. 9:9, Jer. 49:16, Ob. 3, Mk. 7:22 and 1 Jn. 2:16)

An Uncircumcised Heart = A heart that has not been cut, indicating a cleansing from sin, and made pure. (Lev. 26:41, Jer. 9:26, Eze. 44:7-9 and Acts 7:51) Many were circumcised the eighth day after birth, but the real issue of life and relationship with God is a circumcised heart. (Deut. 10:16, Rom. 2:25-29, and Col. 2:11). On Calvary, Jesus was cut in His heart by a Roman soldier. (Jn. 19:34 and Acts 2:37) They were pricked (cut) in their hearts. Without circumcision of the heart, we easily go astray from God's presence and fail to possess heavenly hearts, as required.

This is extremely serious, because Judgment Day is coming and we all shall stand trial for Jesus Christ and be found guilty of these three charges:
1) Loving the Lord with all our hearts,
2) Saved and born again by the blood of the cross, and
3) Having our names written in the Lamb's book of life.

THE ENDING

The word end or ending, *telas* (or teleo) to mean a fulfilment, to complete, finish, to cause activities to cease, such as the end of the world, the end of time, or these last days. Ordinarily (usually, commonly or as a rule) unto every beginning there is an ending, yet, the *Heart of the Cross* has no end but will stand wide open unto all people regardless of ethnic background, belief, sin , or way of life. All must come to spiritual life by the way of the cross. From the beginning, God has set man's ending in place upon the earth, and the Lord shall return in a time that only He knows the day or the hour. This book came forth from God's great heart to my heart for every heart upon the earth to be properly focused and set in the right place and position, waiting for His soon return.

Behold, he cometh with clouds, and every eye shall see him, and they also who pierced (stabbed, penetrated) *him; and all kindreds of the earth shall wail* (cry, weep, moan, howl and lament) *because of him. Even so, amen. I am Alpha and Omega, the beginning and the ending, saith the Lord who is, and who was, and who is to come, the Almighty.* (Rev. 1:7-8). (See Ps. 22:16, Zech. 12:10, Jn. 19:34-37 and Rev. 1:1-3).

Yet the Apostle John saw Him in the beginning as the eternal word (God the Word), incarnate in the Son of God, and wrote in John 1:1 saying: *In the beginning* (inception, origin, start, point of time or place) *was the Word and the Word was with God and the Word was God. The same was in the beginning with God. All things were made by him, and without him was not anything made that was made;* and verse 14 says: *And the Word was made flesh, and dwelt among us and we beheld his glory, the glory as of the only begotten of the Father, full of grace and truth:* and verse 29 says: *The next day John seeth Jesus coming unto him, and saith, Behold the Lamb of God* (God's sacrifice, our replacement, blood donor and sin offering), *who taketh away the sin of the world.*

While all sin would be finished, executed, terminated, and brought to an end by the cross of Jesus Christ, we must remember that the root place and power of sin is the heart of man, and that the Lamb of God was slain from the foundation of this world (Rev. 13:8). The true issue between God and man was/is the issue of the heart, which is the real power and factor of all sinful operations in the earth, from the beginning to the ending. In Genesis 6:5-6, we can see clearly what God saw that caused Him to send a flood upon the earth. *And God saw that the wickedness of man was great in the earth, and that every imagination of the <u>thoughts of his heart</u> was only evil continually. And it repented the Lord that he had made man on the earth, and it grieved him <u>at his heart</u>*. His great heart became sorrowful, anguished, suffering with despair, as a heartache agony that was painful and disturbing. He spoke judgement upon the whole earth, brought forth a flood, and all died except for Noah and his family.

In these end times, mankind judges bodies and things, but God judges hearts and minds. Judgment means to discern for a decision, appraisal, inspection, evaluation, analysis (spiritual inquiry and observation to bring to a conclusion): Both the judgement seat of Jesus Christ for believers and the White Throne Judgment for lost sinners are divine judgments of men's hearts. For we all must appear before the judgment seat of Christ (Rom. 14:8-12), that everyone may receive the things done in his body, according to what he hath done, whether it be good or bad. (2 Cor. 5:10). (See Heb. 9:22-28 and Rev. 20:11-15).

This is (was) the greatest trial that has ever been recorded, in that the innocent died for the guilty who crucified Him, which included the whole world.

After every heart operation, the presiding physician must close up the opening wound so that the heart may heal without danger of an infection. As you close this book, I humbly ask that you continue to look upon the *Heart of the Cross* (even your own heart) to see what the Lord has done!

Other books by the author:

Marriage from the Heart
ISBN-9781615790821
https://www.christianbook.com/marriage-from-the-heart/donald-downing/9781615790821/pd/790821

The Pen of a Ready Writer
ISBN-9781498447522
https://www.christianbook.com/the-pen-of-a-ready-writer/donald-downing/9781498447522/pd/447528

Born In His Image, Birthed in His Likeness
ISBN-9781607910954
https://www.christianbook.com/born-in-his-image-birthed-likeness/donald-downing/9781607910954/pd/910954

Heart Almanac Expository and Curriculum
ISBN-9781606476895
https://www.christianbook.com/heart-almanac-expository-and-curriculum/donald-downing/9781606476895/pd/476895

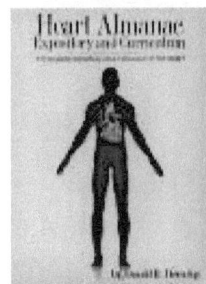

Jael the Conqueror
ISBN-9781615792153
https://www.barnesandnoble.com/w/jael-the-conqueror-bishop-donald-r-downing/1018885675

Hidden Treasures of the Heart
ISBN-978-1560433156
https://www.amazon.com/Hidden-Treasures-Heart-Donald-Downing/dp/1560433159/

The Power of Opinions
ISBN-978-1498447508
https://www.amazon.com/Power-Opinions-Bishop-Donald-Downing-ebook/dp/B0160A5PMQ

Code Red
ISBN-9781597810258
https://www.amazon.com/Code-Red-Donald-R-Downing/dp/1597810258

Code Blue
ISBN-978-0768429701
https://www.amazon.com/Code-Blue-Donald-Downing/dp/0768429706